Ethno-Ecology of Indian Tribes

Ethno-Ecology of Indian Tribes

Diversity in Cultural Adaptation

Amitabha Sarkar
Samira Dasgupta

RAWAT PUBLICATIONS
Jaipur and New Delhi

ISBN 81-7033-631-7

Published by
Prem Rawat for *Rawat Publications*
Satyam Apartments, Sector 3, Jain Temple Road,
Jawahar Nagar, Jaipur - 302 004 (India)
Phone: 0141 651748 / 657006 Fax: 0141 651748
e-mail : rawatbooks@pinkline.net

Delhi Office
G-4, 4832/24, Ansari Road, Daryaganj, New Delhi 110 002
Phone: 011-3263290

Typeset by Rawat Computers, Jaipur
Printed at Nice Printing Press, New Delhi

Contents

Contents

Preface

Tribal culture flourishes in the specific ecological niche. The present volume deals with the Indian tribal situation in varied geographical settings. How natural environment plays an important role in the formation of tribal culture in different eco-settings is the main focus of the study. The traditional knowledge of treatment of various diseases and the conservation of biodiversity as well as cognisance of their environment are also discussed in the perspective of ethno-science of the tribal people of India. At the end of this book, the authors have tried to depict how eco-friendly development planning and programme could be possible in the light of the existing ecological conditions. To understand this situation, selected tribes from Chotanagpur of Bihar, Bastar of Madhya Pradesh, Malkangiri of Orissa and Andaman and Nicobar are taken as samples in the present treatise.

In writing the book the authors were fortunate enough as they got valuable suggestions from Dr. B.K. Dasgupta, Ex-Deputy Director of Anthropological Survey of India in completion of this volume. The authors are very much grateful to him. The authors are also grateful to Prof. P.K. Bhowmick (Retd.), Department of Anthropology, Calcutta University, Shri B.N. Banerjee, Reader (Retd.), Department of Anthropology, Calcutta University, Prof. A.K. Danda, Asiatic Society, Calcutta and Dr. Amal Kumar Das, Ex-Director, Cultural Research Institute, West Bengal who helped by extending their important academic inputs. The authors also express their sincere gratitude to the Director, Anthropological Survey of India, for giving opportunity to visit different tribal pockets in the country in connection with the official assignments, from time to time.

Thanks are also due to Shri Atish Chandra Bhattacharya, Headmaster of Azadgarh Vidyapith of Regent Park, Calcutta and Dr. Jyotrimoy Chakraborty of Anthropological Survey of India, Calcutta for their academic suggestions. The authors also express their sincere thanks to Dr. Vijoy Sahay and Shri. A.P. Nandan for using their published data on Nicobarese. Lastly, the authors feel very grateful to the real patron in preparation of the manuscript—*The Tribal People of Bastar*, with whom they had spent a lot of time during their stay at Bastar.

The authors acknowledge with gratitude and thanks, the active help and cooperation of so many well-wishers without whom the present volume would never see the light of day. Our sincere labour will be amply rewarded if the book serves the purposes of those for whom only it is prepared and presented.

1

Introduction

The socio-cultural anthropologists of the modern age hold that ecological approach is fruitful to understand man, his society and culture. Cultural ecology points that there is an intimate relationship between culture and its surrounding environment. "Interaction between living organisms and their environments are the subject matter of ecological studies" (Vayda, 1968). The total environment is inclusive of both the controlled and uncontrolled environment. Man has a control over a part of environment while a part of it is not amenable to his control and, hence, is called the uncontrolled environment which is otherwise known as geographical environment to which man tries to adapt and adjust himself. The controlled environment is otherwise known as the social environment. In fact, the environment is the sum total of the social environment and the geographical environment.

Man is influenced by his environment and, in turn, influences the environment. The constantly increasing scientific inventions are gradually giving man ever new triumphs over nature and at present he is in a position to control much of the geographical environment, while the cultural environment is man's own creation.

"On the one hand, it is believed that the environment determines a culture (Semple, 1911), and on the other hand, it is expected that the environment limits a culture (Kroeber, 1969; Toynbee, 1947; Forde, 1934). Nobody can ignore the impact of environment on life and culture and the interrelation and interdependence between man and his environment" (Dasgupta, 1994).

With the above perspective, an attempt has been made to analyse and interpret the data on the mutual interdependence of selected central Indian tribes and their immediate geographical environment. Each ethnic group has its own mechanism to exploit nature and nature also in its turn, shapes the culture of the ethnic group. Ethno-ecological approach will, therefore, be helpful to delineate the strategies adopted by various ethnic groups in interacting with specific ecosystem.

Ecology provides the base for technology. It is the interaction of culture and ecology that depends on the technological capability of all human groups. This technology again determines the level of exploitation of nature which in turn manifests in the perception of ecology. Taking a historical view of the facts, it is possible to draw an evolutionary sequence of development of technology, level of exploitation of natural resources and manifestation of culture. These together can be understood as an expression of techno-cultural efficiency (personal discussions with A.K. Danda, December, 1995).

Wissler (1926) and Kroeber (1939) have both explained culture in terms of interrelationship between man and his ecology. Steward (1955; 1968) has mentioned that there is a close relationship between ecosystem and some parts of culture which he terms as culture-core. Clifford Geertz (1968) Marvin Harris (1966), in their works, followed Steward's concept of cultural ecology, which refers to the techno-environmental determinism.

The present volume primarily aims at studying the ethno-ecology of some Indian tribes. It is a distinctive approach in human ecology that focuses on the conceptions of ecological relationships held by people or culture. All the approaches to ecological anthropology that have been discussed in connection with this aspect are "objective", that is, they study man-environmental relationships from the observer's point of view while another approach to study ecological relationships is from the participants' point of view, which is otherwise known as ethno-ecology or cognitive ethnography, ethno-science, etc. (Hardesty, 1977). Rappaport (1963) calls this "cognised" environment.

II

India is the homeland of 427[*] tribal communities (Singh 1994), having different physical features with livelihood. The tribal population in India is 5,16,28,638 (as per 1981 census) which is equivalent to 7.76 per cent of the total population in India.

There are various welfare measures and safeguards for the tribal population in India. According to Article 342 of our Constitution, the tribal people are entitled to have development benefits, provided they are considered as scheduled. The President of India by his special power had declared some groups in various pockets of our country as

---

[*] Singh (1994) has however noted that the number of tribes in India is 461.

"Scheduled Tribe" on 26 January, 1950 and the official definition of Scheduled Tribe is as follows: "Indication of primitive traits, distinctive culture, geographical isolation, shyness of contact with the community at large and backwardness." Similarly, L.M. Shrikant, the first commissioner for Scheduled Castes and Scheduled Tribes has defined Scheduled Tribe as "economically, socially and educationally backward, geographically isolated and remaining outside the Hindu fold".

Before going into depth, let us clarify what we mean by a tribe. We consider that tribe is a group of homogeneous people, that is, with a common way of life and having an in-group sentiment of their own which differentiates themselves from other, having a common geographical territory with a common dialect, usually backward, segmentary society (i.e., specialisation is not rigid and generation-wise), shyness in contact with outsiders, primitiveness in comparison to modern technology, lack of personal ethics in supernaturalism and presence of hierarchic pantheon of their celestial world (like Earth Goddess or *Tallur Muttey* for Bastar region and Sun God or *Sing Bouga* for Chotanagpur region placed at the top) in their worldview and have a belief in the transmigration of soul and reincarnation (Sarkar, 1995). In fact, a tribe is variously conceived by Indian scholars. When a sufficient number of these Scheduled Tribes are confined at one place having more than 50 per cent population, this area is known as "Scheduled Area" (as per the fifth schedule of Indian Constitution). In such areas, tribals are enjoying some special facilities like rights over land, implementation of various socio-economic development programmes, etc.

Out of long list of tribes, considering the level of literacy, level of technology and relative geographical isolation only 75 tribal groups are considered as "Primitive Tribal Groups"

(PTGs) in India. Textual and empirical observation reflects that they (PTGs) are numerically very small, possess crude technology, and their subsistence economy is mainly depended on the mercy of nature. Some of these PTGs are on the verge of losing their tradition.

Table 1
Primitive Tribal Groups *

1.	Andhra Pradesh	1.	Bodo Gadba
		2.	Bondo Poroja
		3.	Chenchu
		4.	Dongaria Khond
		5.	Gutob Gadaba
		6.	Khond Poroja
		7.	Kolam
		8.	Konda Reddy
		9.	Konda Savara
		10.	Kutia Khond
		11.	Parengi Paroja
		12.	Thoti
2.	Bihar	13.	Asur
		14.	Birhor
		15.	Birjia
		16.	Hill Kharia
		17.	Korwas
		18.	Malpaharia
		19.	Parhaiya
		20.	Sauria Paharia
		21.	Savar
3.	Gujarat	22.	Kathodi
		23.	Kotwalia
		24.	Padhar
		25.	Siddi

Contd...

Contd...

		26.	Kolgha
4.	Karnataka	27.	Jenu Kuruba
		28.	Koraga
5.	Kerla	29.	Cholanaikayan (A Section of Kattunaickans)
		30.	Kadar
		31.	Kattunayakan
		32.	Kurumba
		33.	Koraga
6.	Madhya Pradesh	34.	Abujh Maria
		35.	Baiga
		36.	Bharia
		37.	Hill Korba/Hill Korwa
		38.	Kamar
		39.	Saharia
		40.	Birhor
7.	Maharashtra	41.	Katkaria (Kathodia)
		42.	Kolam
		43.	Maria Gond
8.	Manipur	44.	Marram Naga
9.	Orissa	45.	Bhunjia
		46.	Birhor
		47.	Bondo
		48.	Didayi
		49.	Dongria-Khond
		50.	Juang
		51.	Kharia
		52.	Kutia-Khond
		53.	Lanjia Soura
		54.	Lodha
		55.	Mankidi
		56.	Paudi Bhuyan
		57.	Soura

Contd...

Contd...

10.	Rajasthan	58.	Seharia
11.	Tamil Nadu	59.	Kattu Naickan
		60.	Kota
		61.	Kurumba
		62.	Irula
		63.	Paniyan
		64.	Toda
12.	Tripura	65.	Reang
13.	Uttar Pradesh	66.	Buxa
		67.	Raji
14.	West Bengal	68.	Birhor
		69.	Lodha
		70.	Toto
15.	Andaman & Nicobar Islands	71.	Great Andamanese
		72.	Jarawa
		73.	Onge
		74.	Sentenelese
		75.	Shompen

*   as on 1 June, 1989.

III

The Concept of Cultural Ecology and the Present Work

The present treatise deals with the Indian tribal situation and the varied geographical settings in which the tribes live. Naturally, the differential aspects of their culture have to be explained in terms of their geographical setting. Herein, an attempt has been made to portray the role of ecology in the formation of the tribal cultures of India and to highlight how the resources are exploited by the communities living in hilly, forest, island or plain areas. Interest in this area of research has originated from the exposure of the authors to the tribal groups of Bastar of Madhya Pradesh, adjoining Orissa and of Chotanagpur plateau of Bihar, living in different eco-setting and sustaining a pattern of culture, that is, typically of their own. An island tribe is also taken to substantiate and understand the influence of particular niche on the culture. In every case, our attention has been drawn to the way each group has been exploiting the natural resources of the area and how the geography of the area has influenced the culture.

2

Ecological Anthropology

Ecological anthropology may be defined as the study of the relations among the population dynamics, social organisation and culture of human population and the environment in which they live (Orlove, 1980). "It presents the development of ecological anthropology, not as a smooth accumulation of information and insights, but as a series of stages" (Orlove, 1980). "The first stage is characterised by the work of Steward and White, the second is termed neo-functionalism and neo-evolutionism and third one is called processual ecological anthropology" (Orlove, 1980).

The German-Austrian continental diffusionists are considered superior to British School in their outlook, methodology and ideology. Friedrich Ratzel was one of such scholars in German School. He was basically zoologist but soon he turned towards geography and then to anthropology. He wrote many volumes on anthropo-geography. German School of diffusion owes its origin to Ratzel. He made a clear-cut distinction between territorial geography and social geography which he called as anthropo-geography. According to him, environment plays an important adaptive role. He was nevertheless convinced that people were more influenced by one another than by factors of climate and terrain.

"Anthropologists in America led by Boas questioned the unilinearity of the evolutionary thought and the assumption of progress inherent in evolution" (ibid., 1980). The American diffusionists received idea from their German friends and, therefore, it is said that in the American Culture Area Theory of diffusion was influenced by the Museum Methodology of German School of Diffusion. Boas, the father of American ethnology, was born and educated in Germany. German diffusionists were followers of Culture Circle School or Cultural Historic School, talked about complex form of diffusion of culture but they failed to explain as to why diffusion took place. Here American diffusionists attempted to solve this question. On the basis of empirical researches, they discredited the universal sequences established by the classical evolutionists. They were of view that the empirical researches were evident to refer to that give and take of culture traits and culture complex had taken place through the medium of transport and communication. In order to show the diffusion of cultural traits and complexes, the American diffusionists devised a methodology known as culture area approach. They did not analyse cultural diffusion prevalent all over the world at the same time, instead, they divided the world into different cultural areas on the basis of geographical regions. They were of the opinion that geographical aspects of culture could not be ignored in the study of culture area. Thus, according to them, the concept of culture area reveals geographical area of cultural similarities. Under the influence of geographical categories, the American Museum of Natural History, New York and the Field Museum, Chicago decided simultaneously to use geographical categories instead of evolutionary trends in the museum, in order to get better insight by the museum visitors. The teachers of Boas were trained physicists and mathematicians from whom he learnt many theoretical concepts and applied them in anthropological field. He joined an arctic expedition of Baffinland, North America, as a geographer in 1883-84. With the passage of time, a definite central theme "historical particularism" has come to be associated with Boasion period.

The scholars accepted the interest in cultural process and change but looked more prudently for details of each case of cultural change, examining whether traits were diffused or independently invented and how they were reworked by each culture that adopted them. The school that they formed was named historical particularism. In fact, ecological anthropology emerged from the Boasian School of Historical Particularism.

Steward's work in ecological anthropology due to contact with noted geographer Carl Sauer led him to examine the effect of environment on culture. His method of cultural ecology signifies materialist emphasis. This method entails the study of the relation between certain features of the environment and certain traits of the culture possessed by the people living in that environment. Within the environment, Steward emphasised the quality, quantity and distribution of resources. The aspects of culture that he examined most closely were technology, economic arrangements, social organisation and demography, although he also included other aspects. Steward stressed the fact that the environment influenced only certain elements of a culture, which he termed the "culture-core".

"Leslie White's relation to Boasian tradition was somewhat different. White shared Steward's emphasis on culture as the unit of analysis and his interest in cultural evolution; his partitioning of culture into technological, social and ideological components gave him a materialist stance generally similar to Steward's. White was more concerned with the broad details of evolution than with specific adaptations, however, he also directed relatively little, attention to the influence of environment on particular cultures. Instead he emphasised levels of energy use as the determinant of cultural evolution" (Orlove, 1980).

There are certain fundamental differences in the approaches of White and Steward. The former may be called universal evolutionist who defined cultural evolution culturally (and not biologically) while the later was a multilineal evolutionist who adopted a functional approach to comprehend the interrelationship of ecology, technology and other aspects of culture. White's primary thrust has been on 'technology' whereas Steward's major emphasis has been on 'ecology'. Nevertheless, both represent an American trend to reconsider the importance of evolutionism in the post-1935 era.

In the second stage of ecological anthropology there are two main trends: (i) neo-evolutionists who claimed both White and Steward were correct, and (ii) neo-functionalists who claimed that they were both wrong.

The neo-evolutionists established a series of evolutionary stages and used the notions of specific and general evolution to accommodate Steward's method of cultural ecology to White's work on unilineal evolution (ibid., 1980).

The neo-functionalist school is represented by Marvin Harris and the early work of Andrew Vayda and Roy Rappaport. The term 'neo-functionalism' signifies "the social organisation and culture of specific populations as functional adaptations which permit the populations to exploit their environments successfully without exceeding their carrying capacity" (ibid., 1980). "In general, neo-functionalists explain specific aspects of social organisation and culture in terms of functions which they serve in adapting local populations to their environments" (ibid., 1980).

Both neo-evolutionists and neo-functionalists have examined the mechanisms which link social structure and culture to the environment.

Apart from the neo-evolutionist and neo-functionalist schools, a different approach in the arena of ecological anthropology has begun to emerge. This work will be called "processual ecological anthropology". The use of the term "process" refers to the importance of diachronic studies in ecological anthropology and to the need to examine mechanism of change. The term "processual ecological anthropology" signifying current developments in the field does appear to be new. Important trends are: (a) the examination of the relation of demographic variables and production system, (b) the response of populations to environmental stress, (c) the formation and consolidation of adaptive strategies which follow Barth's early work on the use of the concept of the niche, and (iv) new work in Marxism, including the emerging interest of anthropologists in political economy and structural Marxism (Orlove, 1980).

A number of comprehensive treatments of environmental thinking in anthropology and the environment vs. culture controversy have been complied by cultural anthropologists who have found that an ecological approach is fruitful both in research and teaching (Anderson, 1973; Hardesty, 1977, Vayda and Rappaport, 1968). The framework for these reviews has been provided by some contrasting major schools of thoughts or conceptual approaches, viz., environmental determinism, environmental possibilism, cultural ecology of

Steward, and current ecological anthropology including actor-based model, eco-system-based model, ethno-ecology and systems-ecology model, etc.

Environmental Determinism

In this concept, it is said that environment of a particular area determines its culture directly. The founders of this concept are Ratzel (1889), Semple (1911), etc.

Environmental Possibilism

In this concept, environment limits the possibilities of cultural development but not directly determines the culture of a particular area. Kroeber (1939), Toynbee (1947) and Forde (1934) are the believers of this thought.

Culture Ecology

The founder of the concept is Steward (1955). Ecological anthropology emerged from Boasian school of historical particularism. According to Steward, the interaction between environment and technology is related with the core of culture which includes the population structure, economy, socio-political structure. Before Steward, all the scientists used to limit their concept on the material culture. Geertz (1963) and Harris (1966) also followed the model of cultural ecology developed by Steward.

Ecosystem-based Model

Vayda (1968; 1969) and Rappaport (1968) suggested that instead of studying how cultures are adapted to the environment, attention should be focused on the relationship of specific human population to specific ecosystem. In their view, human beings constitute simply another population

among the many populations of plants and animal species
that interact with each other with the non-living components
(climate, soil, water) of their local ecosystem. Thus, the
ecosystem, rather than culture, constitutes the fundamental
unit of analysis in their conceptual framework for human
ecology.

Actor-based Model

The adaptation occurs primarily at the individual level rather
than at the level of group, population and social system. The
founder of this model is Benjamin Orlove (1980). This model
emphasised the process by which the people make decision
about how to interact with their environment.

System Model

A major scientific development in recent years has been the
formulation of "General Systems Theory" which is concerned
with the general properties of the structures and functions of
systems as such rather than with their specific contents;
adaptation and selection through interaction between
ecosystem and social systems (Greetz, 1963; Rambo, 1983).
Ecosystem includes water, soil, climate, flora, fauna, fish, pet
livestock, crops, trees, etc., and social system includes social
organisation, nutrition, health, population, technology,
economy, religious values, language etc. In the system model
of human ecology, both the social system and the ecosystem
with which the population interacts retain their integrity as
systems, with each changing its structural configuration
according to its internal dynamics.

Ethno-ecology

The differences between the approach and philosophy

adopted by ethno-ecology and by systems ecology orientation in anthropology are so great as to make it appear, perhaps, inappropriate to discuss them under the same heading. Ethno-ecologists have produced detailed and excellent data on how people in different societies categorise their environment (Conklin, 1954; Frake, 1962). Vayda and Rappaport (1968) also are in favour of an ethno-ecological approach. Ethno-ecology is essentially a research strategy and a number of anthropologists who have used an etic and systematic theoretical orientation have sought to introduce rigour into their fieldwork by adopting in part an ethno-ecological approach (Knight, 1974).

New Ethnography

In the post-1950 era, the anthropologists have been more interested in cognitive anthropology or structural anthropology or new ethnography. The major thrust has been to understand the structure of the culture and to know about the cognitive structuring of the culture. In the formation of culture or the structure of the culture, geography has influenced immensely and therefore, a thorough assessment of cognitive aspect of ecology has been found to be useful for the study of culture. In this, the new ethnography has relied more on the insiders, cognition than an outsiders, interpretation. This often is called as ethno-science.

3

Geographical Setting and Basic Economy of Tribes in India

This chapter has importance because it is the geographical condition that guides and dictates cultural behaviour as well as the economy of a particular community. We know from Ratzel, Boas, Steward and others how the geographical environment plays an eminent role in shaping the economic and cultural pattern of a community or group. In this context, it is important that we make a comparative study of the basic economy of the tribal groups in India distributed in different ecological settings.

Indian subcontinent is composed of cultural mosaic of different ethnic groups with their distinctive cultural identities. After the passage of 50 years of independence, the Indian society is still blighted with some age-old problems of social stigma. People of India are differentiated as high, low, scheduled, non-scheduled, untouchables, etc. And, the Scheduled Castes and Scheduled Tribes continue to occupy the lower most layer of social ranking and economic strata.

In India, there are altogether 461 tribes (Singh, 1994); of

which about 172 are segments. The number of tribes as per Government of India list today, stands at 427. Singh has, however, noted the number of tribes in India as 461 taking into account some major subdivisions of a number of tribal communities. Thereafter, as the state-wise break up has been made, the number has gone up but that is because there are tribal communities who live in more than one state. They are known for their unique ways of living and distinctive cultures, which provide them a distinct identity in the national scene. The tribal scenario in India is full of varieties. Some of them live in forest environment, some in desert, in hilly terrain, in plains, while others in coastal belt or in Island. In fact, the tribes in India live in different ecological settings. According to their distribution, India is divided into three tribal zones, namely, the North-East, Central and Southern. Due to this variation in their habitation, cultural variations are also found. These people generally have a very little knowledge of technological advancement and due to this they are less competent to tame the various environmental hazards. They have to adjust with the local niche with their little traditional knowledge of technology. Their life and culture is constructed to suit their local environment. In this way, various types of cultures have emerged in the Indian cultural scenario.

Sahay (1981), in his study of the Nicobarese, describes how Nicobarese people, who live in deep forest and whose dwellings are in absolute proximity with sea, adjust with their local ecological niche. They are very much different; their cultural life is absolutely different from the cultural life of the tribes who live in plains or in hilly terrain or in desert.

It is again observed that when a community such as Parhaiya or Korwa dwells in more than one ecological settings, in many aspects of culture variations are obvious.

The Parhaiyas live in hills, valley and also in plains, that is, in three different ecological settings. Prasad (1981) in his study discusses that agriculture is practiced mostly by the Parhaiyas who dwell in the plains. It is done on small-scale by the valley dwellers. But, the Parhaiya living in the hilly terrain hardly practise agriculture. It is known that agriculture in hilly terrain is absolutely impossible and for this reason the hill Parhaiya can hardly practise agriculture. As an occupation agriculture is very suitable for the Parhaiyas of the plains and due to this reason they are mostly agriculturists. Here, due to their ecological variation differences in their economic life is observed. Prasad (1981) has also revealed that in their social sphere differences are noticed. In case of the hill-dwellers, the social organisation comprises "*Chata* → *Lat* → *Patti* → *Kurala*, while in the valley it is *Chatai* → *Gowhel* → *Tola* → *Chapparies* and in the plains it is *Gawana* → *Panchgaon* → *Goar* → *Dih* → *Chulha*" (Prasad, 1981). In this way, difference in many spheres of their cultural life is noticed. Similar thing is observed with the Korwa community of the Gumla district of the Chotanagpur region. Geographically Korwas are divided into two groups, namely, the *Diha Korwa* or plain Korwa and the *Paharia Korwa* or the hill Korwa. Occupational variation among these two groups is obvious. The Korwas in the plains do settled cultivation but the hill Korwas are mainly dependent on gathering. They pursue shifting cultivation in incipient form and are engaged in agricultural labour in the plains in the lands of their Korwa and other non-tribal neighbours. This occupational difference has brought about the differences in their social status. The plain Korwas enjoy superior economic and social status. Due to this, those who live in the plains do not like to arrange marriage of their daughters with the Korwas who live in the hills.

Singh (1996) in his exhaustive study on *People of India* described the settlement pattern of the different tribal groups very nicely. He divided their habitation into hilly terrain, plain, coast, desert (arid), semi-arid, high altitude, valley, plateau, island and dense forest (Table 2).

It is observed that there are tribes who live in more than one ecological setting such as Birjia, Korwa, etc. Some of them live in the plateau, some live in the valley and some others live on the hill slopes. In Table 2 and 3, they are put in all these three categories. Due to this repetition one should not calculate the total number of tribes in India from this table.

Generally, the tribal people live in difficult terrain. Among the total 461 tribes (Singh, 1994), majority of them, i.e., 402 live in hilly terrain. Out of these 461 tribes, 226 live in dense forest, 113 live in plateau, 48 live in high altitude, 46 in valleys, 14 in island, 10 in semi-arid region, 21 in coastal region, 1 in desert and 227 in the plains. Previously, it has been mentioned that there are tribal groups that live in the hilly terrain, high altitude, valley, plateau, plain and in dense forest. So, it is understood from the data that though there are 227 tribes living in the plains but their whole group does not live in the plains. Some of their groups live in the plains while some occupy the hilly terrains and dense forests, etc.

Apart from this, occupational categories of Indian tribes are also taken into consideration (Table 3). The table reflects the co-relation between environment and occupation.

Table 3 on occupational categories is an abstract form of the table on economy and occupation in the book on *People of India* (Vol.VII) edited by K.S. Singh (1996). For the present study the authors have selected nine major occupations and four miscellaneous occupations from the original table of the book referred above.

Table 2

Settlement Pattern of Scheduled Tribes of India

S. No.	States	Hilly Terrain	Plains	Coast	Desert (arid)	Semi arid	High Altitude	Valley	Plateau	Island	Dense Forest
1	2	3	4	5	6	7	8	9	10	11	12
01	Andaman and Nicobar	3 (50.0)	1 (16.7)	4 (66.7)	0 (0.0)	0 (0.0)	0 (0.0)	1 (16.7)	0 (0.0)	6 (100.0)	5 (83.3)
02	Lakhadwip	0 (0.0)	0 (0.0)	0 (0.0)	0 (0.0)	0 (0.0)	0 (0.0)	0 (0.0)	0 (0.0)	7 (100.0)	0 (0.0)
03	Mizoram	16 (100.0)	0 (0.0)	0 (0.0)	0 (0.0)	0 (0.0)	0 (0.0)	10 (62.5)	1 (6.3)	0 (0.0)	14 (87.5)
04	Manipur	20 (95.2)	4 (19.0)	0 (0.0)	0 (0.0)	0 (0.0)	2 (9.5)	0 (0.0)	0 (0.0)	0 (0.0)	5 (23.8)
05	Arunachal Pradesh	56 (90.3)	8 (12.9)	0 (0.0)	0 (0.0)	0 (0.0)	7 (11.3)	3 (4.8)	1 (1.6)	0 (0.0)	44 (71.0)
06	Nagaland	14 (77.8)	4 (22.2)	0 (0.0)	0 (0.0)	0 (0.0)	10 (55.6)	0 (0.0)	3 (16.7)	0 (0.0)	14 (77.8)
07	Meghalaya	12 (80.0)	5 (33.3)	0 (0.0)	0 (0.0)	0 (0.0)	3 (20.0)	1 (6.7)	7 (46.7)	0 (0.0)	8 (53.3)
08	Sikkim	7 (100.0)	0 (0.0)	0 (0.0)	0 (0.0)	0 (0.0)	2 (28.6)	1 (14.3)	0 (0.0)	0 (0.0)	0 (0.0)
09	Assam	12 (38.7)	26 (83.9)	0 (0.0)	0 (0.0)	0 (0.0)	0 (0.0)	2 (6.5)	1 (3.2)	0 (0.0)	5 (16.1)
10	Tripura	18 (94.7)	1 (5.3)	0 (0.0)	0 (0.0)	0 (0.0)	0 (0.0)	1 (5.3)	0 (0.0)	0 (0.0)	12 (63.2)
11	Jammu & Kashmir	4 (57.1)	0 (0.0)	0 (0.0)	1 (14.3)	1 (14.3)	6 (85.7)	0 (0.0)	2 (28.6)	0 (0.0)	0 (0.0)
12	Himachal Pradesh	12 (92.3)	0 (0.0)	0 (0.0)	0 (0.0)	0 (0.0)	9 (69.2)	4 (30.8)	0 (0.0)	0 (0.0)	3 (23.1)
13	Orissa	32 (57.1)	21 (37.5)	0 (0.0)	0 (0.0)	0 (0.0)	0 (0.0)	2 (3.6)	22 (39.3)	0 (0.0)	9 (16.1)
14	West Bengal	8 (28.6)	21 (75.0)	0 (0.0)	0 (0.0)	0 (0.0)	3 (10.7)	4 (14.3)	6 (21.4)	0 (0.0)	10 (35.7)

Contd...

Contd...

15	Bihar	9 (34.6)	15 (57.7)	0 (0.0)	0 (0.0)	0 (0.0)	0 (0.0)	2 (7.7)	17 (65.4)	0 (0.0)	3 (11.5)
16	Uttar Pradesh	2 (40.0)	2 (40.0)	0 (0.0)	0 (0.0)	0 (0.0)	2 (40.0)	0 (0.0)	0 (0.0)	0 (0.0)	3 (60.0)
17	Andhra Pradesh	13 (30.2)	30 (69.8)	8 (18.6)	0 (0.0)	2 (4.7)	1 (2.3)	5 (11.6)	11 (25.6)	1 (2.3)	16 (37.2)
18	Kerala	6 (17.6)	31 (91.2)	1 (2.9)	0 (0.0)	0 (0.0)	0 (0.0)	0 (0.0)	1 (2.9)	0 (0.0)	18 (52.9)
19	Tamil Nadu	11 (39.3)	18 (64.3)	1 (3.6)	0 (0.0)	0 (0.0)	2 (7.1)	4 (14.3)	8 (28.6)	0 (0.0)	16 (57.1)
20	Pondichery	0 (0.0)	0 (0.0)	0 (0.0)	0 (0.0)	0 (0.0)	0 (0.0)	0 (0.0)	0 (0.0)	0 (0.0)	0 (0.0)
21	Karnataka	0 (0.0)	11 (61.1)	0 (0.0)	0 (0.0)	0 (0.0)	0 (0.0)	0 (0.0)	8 (44.4)	0 (0.0)	5 (27.8)
22	Maharashtra	27 (51.9)	32 (61.5)	3 (5.8)	0 (0.0)	3 (5.8)	0 (0.0)	4 (7.7)	19 (36.5)	0 (0.0)	12 (23.1)
23	Goa	0 (0.0)	0 (0.0)	0 (0.0)	0 (0.0)	0 (0.0)	0 (0.0)	0 (0.0)	0 (0.0)	0 (0.0)	0 (0.0)
24	Madhya Pradesh	47 (64.4)	26 (35.6)	0 (0.0)	0 (0.0)	0 (0.0)	1 (1.4)	1 (1.4)	4 (5.5)	0 (0.0)	19 (26.0)
25	Gujarat	18 (64.3)	9 (32.1)	1 (3.6)	0 (0.0)	2 (7.1)	0 (0.0)	0 (0.0)	0 (0.0)	0 (0.0)	5 (17.9)
26	Dadra	0 (0.0)	6 (100)	0 (0.0)	0 (0.0)	0 (0.0)	0 (0.0)	0 (0.0)	0 (0.0)	0 (0.0)	0 (0.0)
27	Daman	0 (0.0)	0 (0.0)	3 (100.0)	0 (0.0)	0 (0.0)	0 (0.0)	0 (0.0)	0 (0.0)	0 (0.0)	0 (0.0)
28	Rajasthan	3 (23.1)	8 (61.5)	0 (0.0)	0 (0.0)	2 (15.4)	0 (0.0)	1 (7.7)	2 (15.4)	0 (0.0)	0 (0.0)
29	Haryana	0 (0.0)	0 (0.0)	0 (0.0)	0 (0.0)	0 (0.0)	0 (0.0)	0 (0.0)	0 (0.0)	0 (0.0)	0 (0.0)
30	Punjab	0 (0.0)	0 (0.0)	0 (0.0)	0 (0.0)	0 (0.0)	0 (0.0)	0 (0.0)	0 (0.0)	0 (0.0)	0 (0.0)
31	Chandigrah	0 (0.0)	0 (0.0)	0 (0.0)	0 (0.0)	0 (0.0)	0 (0.0)	0 (0.0)	0 (0.0)	0 (0.0)	0 (0.0)
32	Delhi	0 (0.0)	0 (0.0)	0 (0.0)	0 (0.0)	0 (0.0)	0 (0.0)	0 (0.0)	0 (0.0)	0 (0.0)	0 (0.0)
	Total	227 (35.7)	402 (63.3)	21 (3.3)	1 (0.2)	10 (1.6)	48 (7.5)	46 (7.2)	113 (17.8)	14 (2.2)	226 (35.7)

Source: Singh K.S., 1996, *People of India: Identity, Ecology, Social Organization, Economy, Linkages and Development Process, National Series* Vol. VII, Delhi: Oxford University Press and Anthropological Survey of India.

Table 3
Occupational Categories

| States | Major Occupations | | | | | | | | | Miscellaneous Occupation | | | |
| | Hunting & Gathering | Trapping Birds & Animals | Shift-ing Culti-vation | Terrace Culti-vation | Settled Culti-vation | Fishing | Horti-culture | Animal Hus-bandry | Pasto-ralism | Textile Weav-ing | Basket Mak-ing | Mat Weav-ing | Toddy Tapp-ing |
	1	2	3	4	5	6	7	8	9	10	11	12	13
1. Andaman & Nicobar	5 (83.3)	0 (0.0)	0 (0.0)	0 (0.0)	0 (0.0)	5 (83.3)	2 (33.3)	1 (16.7)	0 (0.0)	0 (0.0)	3 (50.0)	2 (33.3)	1 (16.7)
2. Lakshadwip	0 (0.0)	0 (0.0)	0 (0.0)	0 (0.0)	7 (100)	7 (100)	0 (0.0)	0 (0.0)	0 (0.0)	0 (0.0)	0 (0.0)	1 (14.3)	0 (0.0)
3. Mizoram	12 (75)	1 (6.3)	16 (100)	4 (25.0)	8 (50.0)	16 (100)	5 (31.3)	10 (62.5)	0 (0.0)	12 (75.0)	11 (68.8)	0 (0.0)	0 (0.0)
4. Manipur	3 (14.3)	0 (0.0)	11 (52.4)	9 (42.9)	16 (76.2)	5 (23.8)	4 (19.0)	5 (23.8)	0 (0.0)	12 (57.1)	10 (47.6)	1 (4.8)	0 (0.0)
5. Arunachal	40 (64.5)	7 (11.3)	44 (71.0)	29 (46.8)	39 (62.9)	40 (64.5)	29 (46.5)	35 (56.5)	1 (1.6)	36 (53.1)	32 (51.6)	6 (9.7)	0 (0.0)
6. Nagaland	10 (55.6)	5 (27.8)	11 (61.1)	13 (72.2)	6 (33.3)	11 (61.1)	8 (44.4)	13 (72.2)	0 (0.0)	12 (66.7)	9 (50.0)	5 (27.8)	0 (0.0)
7. Meghalay	5 (33.3)	1 (6.7)	8 (53.3)	7 (46.7)	11 (73.3)	7 (46.7)	4 (26.7)	9 (60.0)	0 (0.0)	5 (33.3)	8 (53.3)	8 (53.3)	0 (0.0)
8. Sikkim	0 (0.0)	0 (0.0)	0 (0.0)	4 (57.1)	2 (28.6)	0 (0.0))	1 (14.3)	2 (28.6)	0 (0.0)	2 (28.6)	2 (28.6)	1 (14.3)	0 (0.0)

Contd...

Contd...

	C1	C2	C3	C4	C5	C6	C7	C8	C9	C10	C11	C12	C13
9. Assam	2 (6.5)	2 (6.5)	8 (25.8)	3 (9.7)	26 (83.9)	8 (25.8)	5 (16.1)	12 (38.7)	0 (0.0)	11 (35.5)	10 (32.3)	2 (6.5)	1 (3.2)
10. Tripura	3 (15.8)	0 (0.0)	15 (78.9)	0 (0.0)	13 (68.4)	1 (5.3)	2 (10.5)	11 (57.9)	0 (0.0)	0 (0.0)	0 (0.0)	0 (0.0)	0 (0.0)
11. Jammu & Kashmir	0 (0.0)	0 (0.0)	0 (0.0)	0 (0.0)	0 (0.0)	0 (0.0)	1 (14.3)	1 (14.3)	0 (0.0)	0 (0.0)	0 (0.0)	0 (0.0)	0 (0.0)
12. Himachal Padesh	0 (0.0)	0 (0.0)	0 (0.0)	11 (84.6)	1 (7.7)	0 (0.0)	2 (15.4)	7 (53.8)	3 (23.1)	1 (7.7)	1 (7.7)	0 (0.0)	0 (0.0)
13. Orissa	18 (32.1)	5 (8.9)	14 (25.0)	3 (5.4)	42 (75.0)	7 (12.5)	6 (10.7)	21 (37.5)	0 (0.0)	4 (7.1)	7 (12.5)	3 (5.4)	0 (0.0)
14. West Bengal	8 (28.6)	1 (3.6)	1 (3.6)	4 (14.3)	19 (67.9)	3 (10.7)	9 (32.1)	9 (32.1)	0 (0.0)	2 (7.1)	1 (3.6)	1 (3.6)	0 (0.0)
15. Bihar	16 (61.5)	5 (19.2)	4 (15.4)	0 (0.0)	24 (92.3)	5 (19.2)	0 (0.0)	2 (7.7)	0 (0.0)	1 (3.8)	4 (15.4)	1 (3.8)	0 (0.0)
16. Uttar Pradesh	0 (0.0)	0 (0.0)	0 (0.0)	1 (20.0)	5 (100)	0 (0.0)	1 (20.0)	4 (80.0)	0 (0.0)	1 (20.0)	0 (0.0)	0 (0.0)	0 (0.0)
17. Andhra Pradesh	16 (37.2)	1 (2.3)	16 (37.2)	6 (14.0)	33 (76.7)	9 (20.9)	5 (11.6)	18 (41.9)	2 (4.7)	1 (2.3)	5 (11.6)	2 (4.7)	0 (0.0)
18. Kerala	6 (17.6)	12 (35.3)	3 (8.8)	3 (8.8)	24 (70.6)	6 (17.6)	0 (0.0)	20 (58.8)	5 (14.7)	0 (0.0)	11 (32.4)	8 (23.5)	0 (0.0)
19. Tamil Nadu	7 (25.0)	5 (17.9)	1 (3.6)	2 (7.1)	18 (64.3)	4 (14.3)	4 (14.3)	12 (42.9)	3 (10.7)	0 (0.0)	4 (14.3)	2 (7.1)	0 (0.0)
20. Pondichery	0 (0.0)	0 (0.0)	0 (0.0)	0 (0.0)	0 (0.0)	0 (0.0)	0 (0.0)	0 (0.0)	0 (0.0)	0 (0.0)	0 (0.0)	0 (0.0)	0 (0.0)
21. Karnataka	1 (5.6)	0 (0.0)	0 (0.0)	0 (0.0)	14 (77.8)	1 (5.6)	0 (0.0)	4 (22.2)	0 (0.0)	1 (5.6)	5 (27.8)	1 (5.6)	0 (0.0)
22. Maharashtra	16 (30.8)	7 (13.5)	0 (0.0)	3 (5.8)	41 (78.8)	14 (26.9)	3 (5.8)	11 (21.2)	5 (9.6)	1 (1.9)	5 (9.6)	4 (7.7)	1 (1.9)
23. Goa	0 (0.0)	0 (0.0)	0 (0.0)	0 (0.0)	0 (0.0)	0 (0.0)	0 (0.0)	0 (0.0)	0 (0.0)	0 (0.0)	0 (0.0)	0 (0.0)	0 (0.0)
24. M.Pradesh	7 (9.6)	1 (1.4)	6 (8.2)	0 (0.0)	56 (76.7)	5 (6.8)	1 (1.4)	6 (8.2)	0 (0.0)	6 (8.2)	1 (1.4)	1 (1.4)	1 (1.4)

Contd...

Contd...

25. Gujarat	0 (0.0)	0 (0.0)	0 (0.0)	0 (0.0)	18 (64.3)	3 (10.7)	0 (0.0)	0 (0.0)	1 (3.6)	0 (0.0)	3 (10.7)	0 (0.0)	0 (0.0)
26. Dadra	0 (0.0)	1 (16.7)	0 (0.0)	2 (33.3)	2 (33.3)	1 (16.7)	0 (0.0)	0 (0.0)	1 (16.7)	0 (0.0)	0 (0.0)	0 (0.0)	1 (16.7)
27. Daman	0 (0.0)	0 (0.0)	0 (0.0)	0 (0.0)	1 (33.3)	1 (33.3)	0 (0.0)	0 (0.0)	0 (0.0)	0 (0.0)	0 (0.0)	0 (0.0)	0 (0.0)
28. Rajasthan	1 (0.6)	0 (0.0)	0 (0.0)	0 (0.0)	10 (92.3)	0 (0.0)	0 (0.0)	0 (0.0)	0 (0.0)	0 (0.0)	2 (15.4)	0 (0.0)	0 (0.0)
29. Haryana	0 (0.0)	0 (0.0)	0 (0.0)	0 (0.0)	0 (0.0)	0 (0.0)	0 (0.0)	0 (0.0)	0 (0.0)	0 (0.0)	0 (0.0)	0 (0.0)	0 (0.0)
30. Punjab	0 (0.0)	0 (0.0)	0 (0.0)	0 (0.0)	0 (0.0)	0 (0.0)	0 (0.0)	0 (0.0)	0 (0.0)	0 (0.0)	0 (0.0)	0 (0.0)	0 (0.0)
31. Chandigrah	0 (0.0)	0 (0.0)	0 (0.0)	0 (0.0)	0 (0.0)	0 (0.0)	0 (0.0)	0 (0.0)	0 (0.0)	0 (0.0)	0 (0.0)	0 (0.0)	0 (0.0)
32. Delhi	0 (0.0)	0 (0.0)	0 (0.0)	0 (0.0)	0 (0.0)	0 (0.0)	0 (0.0)	0 (0.0)	0 (0.0)	0 (0.0)	0 (0.0)	0 (0.0)	0 (0.0)
Total	175 (27.5)	54 (8.5)	158 (24.8)	104 (16.4)	438 (68.9)	159 (25.0)	84 (13.2)	213 (33.5)	21 (3.3)	102 (16.0)	139 (21.9)	49 (7.7)	5 (0.8)

Source: Singh K.S., 1996, People of India: Identity, Ecology, Social Organization, Economy, Linkages and Development Process, National Series Vol. VII, Delhi: Oxford University Press and Anthropological Survey of India.

The major occupations are:

(1) Hunting and gathering.

(2) Trapping of birds and animals.

(3) Shifting cultivation.

(4) Terrace cultivation.

(5) Settled cultivation.

(6) Fishing.

(7) Horticulture.

(8) Animal husbandry.

(9) Pastoralism.

The miscellaneous occupations are:

(1) Textile-weaving.

(2) Basket-making.

(3) Mat-weaving.

(4) Toddy-tapping.

Except these occupations, there are other occupations such as business, industry, trade, government service, private service, self-employment, labour, industrial works, miscellaneous occupations such as masonry, wood work, metal work, salt-making, jewellery-making, and all the specialised services are not counted for the present study. There are some reasons behind it. Firstly, the authors have taken those occupations which are directly related with the natural environment. Secondly, in spite of having direct relation with natural environment, occupation such as salt-making is left as there is not a single tribal community which has taken it as one of its occupations. Probable reason for it being the tribals lack adequate knowledge of salt-making.

Wood work, jewellery-making, pottery, terracotta and masonry work, and skin and hide work are not taken into consideration in the present study as there is not a single tribal community involved in these occupations.

Metal work is a broader term used for all types of works associated with various metals. In the present study, there are some tribes which are engaged in iron smelting or whose one of the traditional occupations is iron smelting but as it is not separately mentioned in the table, the authors have deleted metal work from the present table.

Another category of occupation, i.e., labour, is not included in the study. It is true that there are some labour works such as agricultural labour, forest labour, etc., which have connection with local environment but as they are not categorically and separately mentioned in the table, they have not also been included in the present study.

Now, when one takes a glance at the table, it is observed that the tribal communities are engaged in more than one occupation. As for example Birjia, a tribe of Chotanagpur region, does slash and burn or shifting cultivation, hunting, gathering, basketry, etc. So Birjias are put in the table in more than one column. Due to this reason, one should not calculate the total number of tribes of India from this table.

It is observed that the highest number of tribes, that is 438 (68.9%), is engaged in settled cultivation. Animal husbandry is done by 213 (33.5%) tribes. In all, 175 (27.5%) tribes are engaged in hunting and gathering, followed by 159 (29%) in fishing, 158 (24.8%) in shifting cultivation, 139 (21.9%) in basket-making, 104 (16.4%) in terrace cultivation, 102 (16%) in textile-weaving, 84 (13.2%) in horticulture, 54 (8.5%) in trapping of birds and animals, 49 (7.7%) in mat-weaving, 21 (3.3%) in pastoralism, and 5 (0.8%) in toddy-tapping.

If the tables on settlement pattern and occupational categories of the Scheduled Tribes are compared, it is observed that in Andaman and Nicobar Islands, 3 (50%) live in hilly terrain, 1 (16.7%) in plains, 4 (66.7%) on the coast, 1 (16.7%) in valley, 6 (100%) in island and 5 (83.3%) in dense forest. As one takes a look at the occupational categories, it is found that of the total tribes, 5 (83.3%) are engaged in hunting, gathering and fishing, 2 (33.3%) in horticulture and 1 (16.7%) in animal husbandry. Among the miscellaneous occupations, basket-making is done by 3 (50%), mat-weaving by 2 (33.3%) and toddy-tapping by 1 (16.7%) tribe. As their habitat is mainly in the coastal area and the hilly terrain of the island, their ecological condition motivates them to do fishing, hunting and gathering. In Andaman and Nicobar Islands, cane is grown abundantly and is necessary for the basket- and mat-weaving.

In Lakshadweep, all the 7 tribes live in the island. All of them mainly practise fishing and settled cultivation. Mat-weaving is taken by only 1 (14.3%) tribal community.

In Mizoram, there are altogether 16 tribes. All of them live in hilly terrain and 14, among them, live in dense forest, 10 in valley and 1 in plateau. All the 16 (100%) tribes in the state are engaged in shifting hill cultivation and depend on fishing for their livelihood, which is done by them in the river flowing through their territory, 12 (75%) do hunting and gathering, 10 (62.5%) pursue animal husbandry, 8 (50%) are engaged in settled cultivation and 4 (25%) in terrace-cum-settled cultivation. Five (31.3%) tribal communities are horticulturists and 1 (6.3%) community traps birds and animals. Among the miscellaneous occupations, textile-weaving and basket-making are done by the tribes of this state. In all, 12 (75%) tribes are involved in textile-weaving and 11 (68.8%) in making baskets.

In Manipur, of the total 23 tribes, 20 (95.2%) reside in hilly terrain, 5 (23.8%) in dense forest, 4 (19%) in plains, and 2 (9.5%) at high altitude. Occupation-wise it is found that majority, that is, 16 (76.2%) of them are settled cultivators, 11 (52.4%) practise shifting hill cultivation, 9 (42.9%) terrace cultivation, 5 (23.8%) each are engaged in fishing and animal husbandry, 4 (19%) horticulture, and 3 (44.3%) in hunting and gathering. Of the miscellaneous occupations, textile-weaving is done by 12 (57.1%), basket-making by 10 (47.6%) and mat-weaving by 1 (4.8%) community only.

In Arunachal Pradesh, there are 67 tribes in all, of which 56 (90.3%) dwell in hilly terrain, 44 (71%) in dense forest, 8 (12.9%) in plains, 7 (11.3%) at high altitude, 3 (4.8%) in valley and 1 (1.6%) in plateau. Adjusting with their ecological setting they mainly practise shifting cultivation, hunting, gathering and fishing. Among them 44 (71%) pursue shifting cultivation and 40 (64.5%) each are engaged in hunting, gathering and fishing. Besides, 39 (62.9%) are engaged in settled cultivation, 35 (56.5%) in animal husbandry, 29 (46.8%) in terrace cultivation and horticulture, 7 (11.3%) in trapping of birds and animals and 1 (1.6%) in pastoralism. Of the miscellaneous occupations, 36 (58.1%) are involved in textile-weaving, 32 (51.6%) in basket-making and 6 (9.7%) in mat-weaving.

In Nagaland, there are altogether 20 tribes distributed in its hilly terrain, dense forest, high altitude, plains and plateau. Among them 14 (77.8%) tribes live in hilly terrain as well as dense forest, while 10 (55.6%) live at high altitude, 4 (22.2%) in plains and 3 (16.7%) in valley. In the state, the maximum number of tribes, i.e., 13 (72.2%) are engaged in terrace cultivation and animal husbandry, followed by 11 (61.1%) in shifting cultivation and fishing, 10 (55.6%) in hunting and gathering, 8 (44.4%) in horticulture and 5 (27.8%) in trapping of birds and animals. Of the miscellaneous occupations, textile-weaving is done by 12 (66.7%), basket-making by 9 (50%) and mat-weaving by 5 (27.8%) tribes.

In Meghalaya, there are 14 tribal groups in total. Of them 12 (80%) are distributed in hilly terrain, 8 (53.3%) in dense forest, 7 (46.7%) in plateau, 5 (33.3%) in plains, 3 (20%) at high altitude and 1 (6.7%) in valley. In case of their occupational categories it is found that 11 (73.3%) pursue settled cultivation, 9 (60%) animal husbandry, 8 (53.3%) shifting cultivation, 7 (46.7%) terrace cultivation, 7 (46.7%) fishing, 5 (33.3%) hunting and gathering, 4 (26.7%) horticulture and 1 (6.7%) trapping of birds and animals. Among the miscellaneous occupations, while basket-making and mat-weaving are done by 8 (53.3%) tribal communities, textile-weaving is done by 5 (33.3%) communities.

In Sikkim, on the whole, there are 7 tribes. More than half of them, i.e., 4 (57.1%) live in hilly terrain, 2 (28.6%) live at high altitude and 1 (14.3%) in valley. The number of tribes engaged in various occupations is same: 4 (57.1%) are engaged in terrace cultivation, 2 (28.6%) in settled cultivation and animal husbandry and 1 (14.3%) in horticulture. Two communities (28.6%) have both textile-weaving and basket-making as their primary occupation.

In Assam, of the 29 tribal groups, 26 (83.9%) reside in the plains, 12 (38.7%) in hilly terrain, 5 (16.1%) in dense forest, 2 (6.5%) in valley and 1 (3.2%) in plateau. It is observed that 26 (83.9%) do settled cultivation, 12 (38.7%) animal husbandry, 8 (25.8%) shifting cultivation and fishing, 5 (16.1%) horticulture, 3 (9.7%) terrace cultivation and 2 (6.5%) hunting, gathering and trapping. Out of the total 29,

11 (35.5%) practise textile-weaving, 10 (32.2%) basket-making, 2 (6.5%) mat-weaving, and 1 (3.2%) toddy-tapping.

In Tripura, of the total 20 tribes, 18 (94.7%) live in hilly terrain, 12 (63.2%) in dense forest and 1 (5.3%) each in plains and in the valley region of the state. It is found that maximum number, that is, 15 (78.9%) of them pursue shifting cultivation, 13 (68.4%) settled cultivation, 11 (57.9%) animal husbandry, 3 (15.8%) hunting and gathering, 2 (10.5%) horticulture and 1 (5.3%) fishing, as their primary occupation.

In all the states of North-East India, there are many rivers. So, fishing is a major source of earning in these states. Textile-weaving, basket-making and mat-weaving as miscellaneous occupations are pursued at all the places, as the necessary raw materials for these jobs such as cane, cocoon and mat grass, are abundantly found in the jungles of these states. In all these states, similar occupational categories are found.

In Jammu & Kashmir, there are 11 tribes; out of which 6 (85.7%) dwell at high altitude, 4 (57.1%) in hilly terrain, 2 (28.6%) in plateau, and 1 (14.3%) each in desert (arid) and semi-arid places. Among the occupations stated in this Table 3, only horticulture and animal husbandry are done by 1 (14.3%) of the tribes.

In Himachal Pradesh, there are altogether 13 tribes. Out of these, 12 (92.3%) live in hilly terrain, 9 (69.2%) at high altitude, 4 (30.8%) in valley and 3 (23.1%) in dense forest. A maximum of tribes, that is, 11 (84.6%) pursue terrace cultivation, followed by 7 (53.8%) animal husbandry, 3 (23.1%) pastoralism, 2 (15.2%) horticulture and 1 (7.7%) settled cultivation.

In Orissa, of the total 54 tribal groups, 32 (57%) live in hilly terrain, 22 (39.3%) in plateau, 21 (37.5%) in plain, 9 (16.1%) in dense forest and 2 (3.6%) in valley. It is observed that maximum number of tribal people, that is, 42 (75%) practise settled cultivation. Besides, 21 (37.5%) are engaged in animal husbandry, 18 (32.1%) in hunting and gathering, 14 (25%) in shifting cultivation, 7 (12.5%) in fishing, 6 (10.7%) in horticulture, and 5 (8.9%) in trapping of birds and animals. Among the miscellaneous occupations, basket-making is done by 7 (12.5%), 4 (7.1%) are involved in textile-weaving, and 3 (5.4%) in mat-weaving.

In West Bengal, similar to Orissa, maximum number of tribes, that is, 19 (67.9%) are involved in settled cultivation. Of the rest, 9 (32.1%) pursue animal husbandry, 8 (28.6%) hunting and gathering, and 3 (10.7%) each fishing and horticulture. Among the miscellaneous occupations, textile-weaving is done by 2 (7.1%), while basket-making and mat-weaving by 1 (3.6%) tribe.

In Bihar, on the whole, there are 26 tribal communities. Out of which 17 (65.4%) live in plateau, 15 (57.7%) live in hilly terrain, 9 (34.6%) in plain, 3 (11.5%) in dense forest and 2 (7.7%) in valley. On the other hand, 24 (92.3%) practise settled cultivation, 16 (61.5%) hunting and gathering, 5 (19.2%) trapping of birds and animals and fishing, 4 (15.4%) shifting cultivation and 2 (7.7%) animal husbandry. Among the miscellaneous occupations, 4 (15.4%) are basket-makers, and 1 (3.8%) each is textile-weaver and mat-weavers.

In Uttar Pradesh, there are 5 tribes in all, of which 3 (60%) reside in dense forest, 2 (40%) in hilly terrain, 2 (40%) each in plains and at high altitude. Apart from settled cultivation, 4 (80%) pursue animal husbandry, and 1 (20%) each terrace cultivation and horticulture. Among the miscellaneous occupations, only textile-weaving is done by 1 (20%) tribe.

In Andhra Pradesh, there are 43 tribes. Out of them 30 (69.8%) live in hilly terrain, 16 (37.2%) in dense forest, 13 (30.2%) in plains, 11 (25.6%) in plateau, 8 (18%) on the coast, 5 (11.6%) in valley, 2 (4.7%) in semi-arid area, and 1 (2.3%) each at high altitude and in island. Occupation-wise, there are 33 (76.7%) tribes which are engaged in settled cultivation, 18 (41.9%) in animal husbandry, 16 (37.2%) in hunting and gathering, 16 (37.2%) in shifting cultivation, 9 (20.9%) in fishing, 6 (14%) in terrace cultivation, 5 (11.6%) in horticulture, 2 (4.7%) in pastoralism, and 1 (2.3%) in trapping of birds and animals. Among the miscellaneous occupations, basket-making is done by 5 (11.6%), whereas mat-weaving by 2 (4.7%) and textile-weaving by 1 (2.3%).

In Kerala, of the 34 tribes in total, 31 (91.2%) reside in hilly terrain, 18 (52.9%) in dense forest, 6 (17.6%) in plains, 1 (2.9%) each on the coast and in plateau. Out of the total tribes, 24 (70.6%) are engaged in settled cultivation, 20 (58.8%) in animal husbandry, 12 (35.3%) in trapping of birds and animals, 6 (17.6%) in fishing, hunting and gathering, 5 (14.7%) in pastoralism, and 3 (8.8%) each in shifting cultivation and terrace cultivation. There are 11 (32.4%) tribes which have taken basket-making as their secondary occupation, and 8 (23.5%) are mat-weavers.

In Tamil Nadu, in all, 24 tribes inhabit. Out of them 18 (64.3%) live in hilly terrain, 16 (57.1%) in dense forest, 11 (39.3%) in plains, 8 (28.6%) in plateau, 4 (14.3%) in valley, 2 (7.1%) at high altitude and 1 (3.6%) on the coast. Likewise, 18 (64.3%) tribes have taken to settled cultivation, 12 (42.9%) to animal husbandry, 7 (25%) to hunting and gathering, 5 (17.9%) to trapping of birds and animals, 4 (14.3%) to fishing, 3 (10.7%) to pastoralism, 2 (7.1%) each to horticulture and terrace cultivation, and 1 (3.6%) to shifting cultivation. Out of the total, 4 (14.3%) pursue basket-making and 2 (7.1%) mat-weaving as their miscellaneous occupation.

In Karnataka, there are 19 tribal groups; of which 11 (61.1%) reside in hilly terrain, 8 (44.4%) in plateau and 5 (27.8%) in dense forest. Occupation-wise, 14 (77.8%) practise settled cultivation, 4 (22.2%) animal husbandry and 1 (5.6%) each fishing and hunting and gathering. Five (27.8%) have taken up basket-making, and 1 (5.6%) each textile-weaving and mat-weaving as miscellaneous occupation.

In Maharashtra, on the whole, there are 47 tribes. Of them 32 (61.5%) live in hilly terrain, 27 (51.9%) in plains, 19 (36.5%) in plateau, 12 (23.1%) in dense forest, 4 (7.7%) in valley, and 3 (5.8%) each in semi-arid land and coastal areas. On the other hand, 41 (78.8%) are engaged in settled cultivation, 16 (30.8%) in hunting and gathering, 14 (26.9%) in fishing, 11 (21.2%) animal husbandry and 7 (13.5%) in trapping of birds and animals. Similarly, 5 (9.6%) have taken up pastrolism, whereas 3 (5.8%) are terrace cultivator and horticulturists. Out of all, 5 (9.6%) are engaged in basket-making, 4 (7.7%) in mat-weaving, and 1 (1.9%) each in textile-weaving and toddy-tapping.

In Madhya Pradesh, of the total 65 tribes, 47 (64.4%) live in plains, 26 (35.6%) in hilly terrain, 19 (26.0%) in dense forest, 4 (5.5%) in plateau, and 1 (1.4%) each at high altitude and in valley. In this state most of the tribal people live in plains adjusting with the ecological condition. Of the total tribes in the state, 56 (76.7%) are associated with settled cultivation, 7 (9.6%) with hunting and gathering, 6 (8.2%) with animal husbandry, 6 (8.2%) with shifting hill cultivation,

5 (6.8%) with fishing, and 1 (1.4%) each with the trapping of birds and animals and horticulture. Of the miscellaneous occupations, 6 (8.2%) have taken to basket-making, and one each (1.4%) to mat-weaving and toddy-tapping.

In Gujarat, a total of 31 tribes inhabit; out of which 18 (64.3%) live in plains, 9 (32.1%) in hilly terrain, 5 (17.9%) in dense forest, 2 (7.1%) in semi-arid region and 1 (3.6%) on the coast. Among the occupational categories mentioned in the table, 18 (64.3%) are involved in settled cultivation, 3 (10.7%) in fishing and 1 (3.6%) in pastoralism. In the state, only 3 (10.7%) have taken up basket-making as their miscellaneous occupation.

In Dadra, there are 6 tribes. All of them live in hilly terrain. Out of them 2 (33.3%) each pursue terrace cultivation and settled cultivation, and 1 (16.7%) each trapping of birds and animals, fishing and pastoralism. One (16.7%) tribe has toddy-tapping as miscellaneous occupation.

There are 3 tribes in Daman living in the coastal region. Out of them 1 (33.3%) each is involved in settled cultivation and fishing.

In Rajasthan, there are 14 tribes in all; of them 8 (61.5%) reside in hilly terrain, 3 (23.1%) in plains, 2 (15.4%) in semi-arid region and 2 (15.4%) in plateau. Among these tribes, 12 (92.3%) have adopted settled cultivation, 1 (0.6%) hunting and gathering and 2 (15.4%) basket-making as miscellaneous occupation.

It is observed from the above analysis that out of total 461 tribal communities, maximum number, that is, 402 (63.3%) live in hilly terrain, 227 (35.7%) in plains, 226 (35.7%) in dense forest, 113 (17.8%) in plains, 48 (7.5%) at high altitude, 46 (7.2%) in valley, 21 (3.3%) on the coast, 14

(2.2%) in island, 10 (1.6%) in semi-arid region and 1 (0.2%) in desert area.

In case of occupations, it is found that the maximum number of tribes, that is, 438 (68.9%) are settled cultivators. It is also true that in maximum number of cases, these people have not much fertile and irrigated land that is really suitable for settled cultivation. Likewise, the maximum number of the tribal people live in the hilly terrain. Most of their land is situated either on the hilltops or slopes where slash and burn or shifting cultivation and terrace cultivation are suitable. But, due to the implementation of Forest Act, shifting cultivation is banned and they are forced to stop shifting cultivation and compelled to shift to settled cultivation even in much unfavourable situation. As they have inadequate knowledge of technology, they hardly can cope with or tackle the unfavourable terrain and hence get less products as compared to what they produced earlier through shifting cultivation. If one observes the comparative analysis in the book, *People of India*, he finds that settled cultivation as a traditional occupation was done by 238 (37.4%) tribes while 227 (35.7%) tribes acquired it later. Twenty-seven (4.2%) have left the occupation for various reasons. There are 402 (63.3%) tribes living in hilly terrain, 48 (7.5%) at high altitude and 46 (7.2%) in valley for whom both shifting and terrace cultivations are easy avenues for earning. It is found that traditionally 228 (35.8%) tribal communities used to practise shifting cultivation, out of which 76 (11.9%) have abandoned. At present, 158 (24.8%) are engaged in shifting cultivation. It is also found that those who still involved in it, in most of the cases (except the Abuj Maria of Bastar among the studied tribe) are doing it very secretly and in incipient form. Hence, this is not sufficient for their livelihood.

Terrace cultivation, as another major and traditional occupation, is done by 48 (7.5%) tribes and now the number has gone up to 104 (16.4%).

Animal husbandry is another such occupation presently adopted by the tribal people on a large scale and 213 (33.5%) of the tribes are engaged in it as a major occupation while traditionally it was done by 135 (21.2%) tribes only.

There are 226 (35.7%) tribes living in dense forest, so hunting and gathering from the jungle have special emphasis in their occupational life. But hunting as an occupation has become obsolete due to the scarcity of wild gang and also due to the restriction on hunting which is declared as illegal. Gathering, as an occupation, still has importance in the tribal economy. There are still 175 (27.5%) tribes involved in this occupation. It is again noticed that among the miscellaneous occupations, basket-making and mat/textile-weaving are frequently done by the tribes, where the raw materials are collected from jungle. There are 139 (21.9%) tribes which have taken up basket-making, 102 (16%) involved in textile-weaving and 49 (7.7%) in mat-weaving. Toddy-tapping is found among only 5 (0.8%) tribes where toddy palm trees are grown abundantly.

It is found that 21 (3.3%) tribes reside on the coast and 14 (2.2%) in island. Except these there are several tribal groups living very close to river and other water sources.

Again, where they have a chance to practise fishing, it becomes one of the major occupations. It is observed that 159 (29%) tribes are engaged in fishing and all of them live very close and around the water sources. Besides, 54 (8.5%) are involved in trapping of birds and animals and 21 (3.3%) are the pastoral people.

Therefore, from the above description, it can be concluded that ecology plays a very important role in shaping the tribal economic life.

4

Environment and Culture

India is a country of cultural diversities that help us to understand the unique quality of its cultural mosaic. But surprisingly, tone of unity is lying behind all these diversities so that India emerges as a composite whole. The people living in this vast area have different ethnic boundaries with different levels of cultural development. These different cultures like different flowers composing a colourful bunch, have merged to one single entity, namely, the Indian civilisation (Banerjee, 1968).

In this chapter, the tribal people of India are seen in the background of their physical environment which moulds and affects their culture. The different modes of cultural behaviour are found among the people living in plains, hills, islands, deserts and forests, etc. In the following lines the tribes are discussed in the context of their physical environment like hills, forests and island, etc.

The tribal people of the Indian subcontinent are indigenous people who have settled in this subcontinent before the Aryan and Dravidian invasions. The tribes of this subcontinent live in diverse eco-settings and as a result their level of development are also found in varying degree. Vidyarthi (1981) has classified the Indian tribal population into seven cultural strata basing on their ecosystem, traditional economy, belief in supernatural power and recent impact. These are as follows: (a) forest hunting, (b) primitive hill cultivation, (c) plain agricultural type, (d) simple artisan group, (e) pastoral and cattle herders, (f) industrial, and (g) urban workers type. In fact, cultures of Indian civilization are highly influenced by the opportunities and limitations offered by the physical environment of the country.

Hill and Forest Tribes

Birjia

The Birjia are a lesser known forest-dwelling primitive tribe, living in the forest clad villages of the Gumla, Lohardaga and the Palamau districts of the Chotanagpur plateau of Bihar and some districts of the Madhya Pradesh. It is told that their original place of habitation is in Madhya Pradesh from where they have come to the present habitat by practising slash-and-burn cultivation in the hills of that region where they had to shift from one field to another after two to three subsequent years of cultivation in the same field.

Elwin, in his book *Agaria* (1991, reprinted), holds that the name Birjia or Birjhia is probably derived from the word "Bewariya", meaning a worker on shifting cultivation; but the people themselves have a different opinion. According to them, in their dialect 'Bir' denotes a fish and 'jia' is a jungle and Birjia altogether means fish of the jungle. In fact, they really feel very comfortable to live in the jungle as a fish remains comfortable in the water.

The Birjia is a very small and scattered tribe numbering only 4,057 (1981 census) people. They live in multi-ethnic villages which are situated in or very close to jungle and their hamlets are always seen isolated from other community's hamlets, generally in the jungle. Their hamlets are situated either on the *ghats* or hill slopes which are clothed with forest and dotted with bamboo grove, or on the *pats* or hilltops. In such a situation, where they are nourished in the lap of nature, their economic activities, social and political organisation, religious manifestation or in a word their whole culture is very much related with their natural environment that is forest environment.

The Birjia hamlets are small and scattered. They live in hilly terrain where the houses cannot be arranged in any particular fashion. They construct their houses with several wooden logs, bamboo and branches of trees. The roof is thatched with a kind of locally available grass, known as *kher* grass. All these things are collected from jungle. They take the help of forest products to construct their houses. *Kher* grass has now been replaced by *khapra* (handmade tile).

Iron smelting, basket-making, *beonra* (slash and burn) cultivation, hunting and collection are their traditional modes of sustenance. With the implementation of Forest Act, *beonra* has been banned by the government. In that situation, they have to start settled cultivation or plough cultivation. Their cultivable land is not suitable for plough cultivation. They do not get a good harvest from their land. In this situation, they could not totally leave their traditional mode of slash and burn cultivation. Now-a-days, they do it but cannot do it on large scale. They have to perform it with a secrecy and in a very incipient form. Iron smelting as an occupation has lost its importance as iron implements of better variety are easily available in the local market on cheaper rates. Only two or three persons, in the studied villages, still indulge in smithery work. It is observed that at presently they have no such occupation which one can identify as their primary occupation, hence they have no fixed occupation. It primarily depends on the occupational opportunity and on the availability of the local resources where again a seasonal variation is marked. In their villages where bamboo—a local forest resource is available—the Birjia are basket-makers. Again, where the bamboo is grown in plenty, and the forest department feels it profitable to employ some workers to cut bamboo for the government, the Birjia in such villages take the opportunity to work under the contractor employed by the government instead of basket-making as the former is a profitable source of income. Those who live in or around wood, they earn their livelihood as wood-cutters. Since they live in and around forest, they collect plenty of edible roots, fruits, tubers, leaves, seeds, etc., from the forest. Everyday they go to forest to collect these items. These items mainly substantiate their daily food chart. Mushroom and young bamboo shoot locally known as *putu* and *bans karil* are very tasty items which are also collected from jungle. There are other items such as *bidi* leaves, sal seed, etc., which they collect and sell in the market to earn cash. So gathering as an occupation cannot be ignored. Today, they hardly can get any animal in the jungle; so hunting as an occupation is quite impossible. It has been told earlier that they are now-a-days forced to take up plough cultivation. Their land is mainly rainfed so that they mostly can cultivate in their land during rainy season. During that period it is difficult to go to forest to cut wood and bamboo and to collect plenty of edibles. The forest sometimes even become inaccessible. Labour, except in the agricultural sector, is also generally withheld during rainy season. So, in that season they have to give priority to their occupation in their agricultural field—on the plough cultivation. So it is obvious that along with occupational opportunity and availability of resources, a seasonal variation in occupation is also marked among them.

The size of the Birjia hamlets depends on the availability of local resources. Where there is plenty of jungle products or occupational opportunity, the size of hamlet is large in comparison to the places with lesser opportunities.

Job opportunity depends on the availability of local resources. So one can say that the local environment, that is, forest environment plays vital role in governing their economic life which again suggest their population number, size of hamlet, etc.

Their food chart is very much enriched with the forest products such as roots, tubers, flowers, leaves, mushroom, honey, etc., which they collect from jungle. Due to their intimate exposure with the immediate forest environment, they have a very good knowledge of the qualities and varieties of all forest products and also know which of them are edible and which not. They know how to cope up with hot summer and severe winter. During summer when they go to jungle, they take with them some rice, water, salt and tamarind in a *tumba* whenever they feel thirsty and hungry they drink water, and take out the rice which is already boiled by this time and take it. The water mixed with salt and tamarind acts as electrol water during summer and it keeps their body cool. They get energy from it and can do hard work in scorching heat.

The tribe is traditionally divided into two endogamous *koms*, namely, the Sinduriya and the Telia or Telha. The Sinduriya claim superiority over the beef-eating Telha. Each of the *kom* is divided into a number of exogamous totemistic *sirthas* or *gotras*. The names of the *sirthas* are identified with the plants and animals of the jungle such as Lakra (leopard), Baghwar (tiger), Bir (a kind of fish), Tatenga (lizard), etc. At present, their traditional patterns of marriage, viz., *kom* endogamy and *sirtha* exogamy are not followed and instead of those they follow *kodaku* or lineage exogamy as their marriage rule.

The Birjia are partrilineal. Sons have the right to inherit their father's property and a daughter can only get the property in the absence of son in the family. In case of succession, it is told that the eldest son gets the authority to do ancestor worship of family in the absence of his father.

They believe that life occurred in the world as a blessing from the 'heavenly father'. Delivery takes place in a separate room which is constructed specifically for this purpose or in a corner of main room, far away from the *ora-bhitar*. One or two midwives locally known as *dagrin* help her to deliver the child. The umbilical cord is cut with a sharp-edged bamboo split locally known as *kamti*. Now it is replaced by a sharp knife. Placenta is buried outside in a corner of the house. A strong string of bark is tied above the navel. The mother and the infant remain polluted upto the day of *chhatti*. Nobody is allowed to touch them, as it makes the other persons also polluted. To become pollution free a polluted person has to get an oil massage with *dori* or *karua* oil. On the sixth or the ninth day after detachment of the dried up umbilical cord from the body of the child, the woman with the infant takes purificatory bath after massaging the whole body with *dori* (mahua) oil and turmeric. The woman washes her head with a locally available clay known as *gili hans*. Traditionally, on the day of *chhatti*, they offer a chicken to their ancestors, in the *ora-bhitar* (the place of their ancestors). The woman cooks it there and offers it to the ancestors. Then, a feast is given to the guests and invitees. Today, due to economic constraint they generally cannot perform all the rituals in time. Some of the practices such as ancestor worship, guest entertainment, etc., are performed later, after three to four months.

Among them, *bia* (marriage by negotiation) is the most preferred type of marriage. The other types of marriage are love marriage or *ghusaghusi*, *qulat* or by exchange, *dhuku or dhakadhuru* or intrusion, *devar tuli* or junior levirate, *sarin biya* or junior sororate, etc. *Sagai* is performed for the widow, separated and divorced persons. Polygyny is allowed, polyandry is not permitted. In a marriage, there are several phases of ritual performances. Among those *tel* or *sindurdalna* (putting of oil or vermilion) on the bride and the bridegroom's forehead are the most important rituals. There are several formalities which are again regarded as parts of the marriage ritual, e.g., *duttam jharra* (ceremonial sending of at least two pots of rice-beer to the bride's house), *ora-neal* (visit by a girl to her would be husband's house), etc.

It is told that they have to spend a lot on marriage. They have a custom of payment of bride-price. They have to entertain guests and invitees. Due to this, now, most of the time, they cannot follow and perform all the rules, regulations and customs. Generally, when a girl goes for *ora-neal* (to see her would be husband's house) she continues to stay there as his wife. In such cases, they can have children also. Putting of vermilion is obligatory, when a community feast also is given. It may be done later but not after their child's marriage. Generally, they perform it as early as possible. Till the performance of this ritual the woman is customarily not included in the family and not allowed to perform and participate in their ancestor worship.

They believe that death occurs due to the malevolent act of evil spirits. They believe that soul of a dead called *mua* never dies. Nobody can see it but can feel it from various experiences of day to day. They have informed that cremation is the rule but burial is also permitted. Now-a-days, they preferably bury the dead instead of going for cremation. It is told that with the implementation of Forest Act, their own right on the forest has come to cease. Wood has became a costly item of economic pursuit. So, they do not want to burn it. Again they opine that if they cremate a dead, they have to perform *gami* or the ritualistic feast within a fortnight. In case of burial, they get a year time to do it. So, at present, burial is generally practised by the tribe.

Birjia life and culture is very much influenced by their local environment, that is, forest environment. It is significant noted from their rituals. Dori oil, extracted from mahua seed, is used for purification of pollution connected with their lifecycle. They tie *boke* (a thread made of bark of a particular tree) on the navel to tie the umbilical cord of a newly born child. Sal wood and bamboo are needed to construct the marriage pandal as these are regarded as very auspicious for that purpose. Sal leaves are also used as plates. They carry a dead body on bamboo bier. They spread a mat over the bier. The mat is weaved by date palm leaves. The dead body is tied with some creeper. Bark of *gambhar* tree and *birni* grass are used as purifiers. There are several other items collected from jungle, used by them in their lifecycle rituals.

Their traditional panchayat of social control at village level is Chota Kutumayat and at inter-village level is Bara Kutumayat. A Chota Kutumayat is headed by a Khuta Madhosh and that of Bara Kutumayat is headed by a Madhosh. As they live in small hamlets, they are not eager to form any permanent structure of social control. Whenever a dispute arises in the society, they immediately form that body temporarily solve the problem and immediately after that the body is dissolved.

They live in hills and in forest surroundings and always with a feeling of insecurity and danger. They think that in the jungle there are numerous malevolent spirits. To avoid them a pregnant woman never goes alone in the forest and take several other protections to avoid the evil spirits. They believe that where there are malevolent spirits such as ghosts, demons, etc., there are also several deities to give them protection from the mischievous acts of those malevolent spirits. These deities reside in the hills, jungles, rivers, streams, etc. So to get their blessings, to get security, they always propitiate all those deities who reside in the natural environment and objects. They believe that if they are displeased, they withdraw their support and leave the people in the world full of insecurity and unknown happenings. Natural calamities may break down in their village. They believe in the supernatural power of nature. Their important rituals are Sarhul, Karma, Kharwaj, Kharihan, Fultuki, etc. Among their deities *sing bonga* or Sun God is very important. It is believed that he lives in Saragpur or heaven and created the world and all the worldly objects. Goreya bonga is the presiding deity of *gohri* or cattleshed. She protects the cattle from all types of diseases and dangers. Gadidara Roeda another deity living in jungle, controls the movement of deers. Whenever a hunting party goes for hunting, the hunters at first worship the deities associated with hunting and forest. They believe that the deity will protect them from all types of dangers in the jungle and the expedition will be successful.

Their sacred place *sarna* is a patch of forest growth and is situated just under a big sal grove, under some big trees. The Birjia perform some of their very important rituals such as Sarhul at that place. Among the other places of worship their cultivable lands are also to be noted. One of the most important sacred place is *ora-bhitar* situated in their household where their deceased ancestors are established. They always keep those sacred places very tidy and never tolerate any inauspicious happening at those places. They are not allowed to destroy or cut any tree in the *sarna* also.

They always think that any type of ailment is caused due to the mischievous act of evil spirits. So, in such conditions, they immediately consult a *deona* or *manti* who through his magico-religious performances detect the real cause and the person or spirit associated with it. Along with it, he suggests some sort of remedies to nullify the effect of evil spirit through his magico-religious performances. The *manti* or *deona* also works as their medicine man. They have much faith in the locally available medicinal herbs, shrubs, etc., which are generally given by the chemist and the knowledgeable persons. These medicinal herbs/shrubs are available in the nearby forests. They do not like to take the advise of the government doctors leaving their own indigenous things found in plenty in their local environment.

Therefore, from the above discussion it is clearly noted that the Birjia life and culture is very much oriented towards their local environment.

Parhaiya

The Parhaiya are one of the most primitive tribal groups of Bihar. They are forest-dwellers, hunting-gathering tribe. They numbered 24,012 as per 1981 census and their rate of literacy was 1.6 percent. They are scattered in hilly and forest tracts of Palamou, Hazaribagh, and Ranchi districts. Their chief concentrations are in Chainpur, Bishrampur, Lathehar, Manika, and Daltongange Sadar block of Palamou district of Bihar. The original habitat of Parhaiya was on the hilltop.

Now many among them are to be found residing in the plain but their choice, till date, is hilly forest area. Some are good cultivators but the majority live in the hill ranges. "According to their own tradition they believe that their forefathers used to reside in *basa bakhar* (bamboo-groves); later on houses were made of khore leaf and bamboos" (O'Malley, 1926).

It is believed that Parhaiya are descendants of Pandawas of the great Hindu epic *The Mahabharat* and hence they are known as Pandawabansi Parhaiya. There is another version according to their own legend that they have originated from *jhalaka* (scare-crow). Later on, the baby was nourished in the hut on deer milk and *kandmul* (tubers, roots etc,). This is why Parhaiya count *kandmul* as their staple food.

The livelihood of Parhiaya is fully influenced by forest environment. The influence of forest is so deep-rooted that they cannot conceive of living away from forest, because they look to the forest as an amicable source of livelihood. Forest helps them in every walk of life. They are dependent on forest to such an extent that their whole economy revolves round the forest. They feel more secured in the surroundings of the forest because it provides them food, shelter, drink, raw materials for hut building, basket weaving and herbal medicines.

The economic activities are still closely interwoven with forest and the economic utility of forest in their life can be understood in the following way:

Forest serves as a source of shelter, food and drink, game, and pasture—it also serves them in supplying indigenous medicine, and raw materials for basketry and hut-making.

The Parhaiya are mainly hunting and food gathering tribe. The men hunt wild animals for their food, while the women with children collect forest produces for their livelihood. The forest products collected are as follows: *gethi, nakoa kanda* (all are wild tubers), leafy vegetables, *madh* (honey) and *khukhundi* (mushroom). With the introduction of Forest Law, the Parhaiya have had to come down and settle at the foot of these hills in the forests. Their economy has received a setback due to strict forest laws. They are now mainly landless and have to depend on labour in the land of neighbouring communities like Chero, Kharwar and Brahman, etc. It is also reported that Parhaiya practised slash and burn cultivation which was known as *parah* or *beoa*. Some among them also practised lac cultivation. Collected honey and *gondh* (gum) from forest are bartered in weekly market with local traders for food grains. They are expert as *kath* or Catechu-makers, bamboo-cutters and Charcoal-makers. They used to sell their produced baskets, winnowing fan, broomsticks, etc., in the weekly market. The raw material for preparing basket, that is, bamboos are collected from local forest.

The basis of social organisation in this territory varies according to the variation in the ecological and social setting. It is again different in western and eastern regions of the district. The territorial organisation in the studied (i.e., northern) region is as follows: *Chulaha → Dih → Gaon → Panchgaon → Gawania*.

The boundary of a *Gawania* runs upto the territorial unit of the erstwhile zamindari estate under which it was operated. All the *gaons* (villages) under such territorial unit are called as *Panchgaon*. Further, a particular *gaon* (village) has many *dihs* (hamlets) having many *chulaha* or households (one hearth is equivalent to one household in the village). The Parhaiya of this region practise socio-religious and economic activities within this territorial boundary. On the whole, a Parhaiya simply **recognises** his territorial and social affiliation with the words *bhat* (rice) and *chatai* (mat), which reflect that a Parhaiya social extension runs upto the limit where he accepts *bhat* and *chatai* for eating and sitting.

In their social organisation, lineage plays a vital role. In such territorial segment the network of kinship ties is given unity and coherence by their common relationship with the dominant lineage that resides there. As these separate lineages are composite in relation to other lineages so the whole tribe is built on agnatic framework. This dominant lineage or the original dwellers of a particular territorial unit is known as *jeth rayat* in the studied area, that is, in northern region at Bisharampur of Palamou District of Bihar. It also speaks that a Parhaiya has two sets of affiliation, viz., the territorial segment and the lineage.

They do not have any clan system and do not function as the totemistic group. So the Parhaiya social organisation may be perceived on the basis of lineage or *khut*. The lineage system and ancestor cult are the centripetal forces. The spirit of the father is sacred and considered along the ancestor spirits. As the lineage and locality are inseparably intermixed in the social structure, so the ancestors are intimately associated with the religion. The original dweller called *jeth rayat* belonging to the dominant lineage and the immigrant lineage members are known as *gaon basua*. It is also reported that the villages were organised on the basis of *khut* (lineage). A *khut kut* had its own territorial unit for habitation. The oldest *khut kut* of the locality was known as *jeth khut* in the northern region. It keeps key position in the village organisation. On the whole, the lineage itself forms three types of groups, namely, dominant lineage (*madasth khut*), the follow-up lineage *khut kut* and immigrant lineages (*gaon basua*). These three groups are interlinked with special reference to authority and solidarity among them. Inside the village the sole authority rests on *madasth khut*, and *khut kut* which plays a pivotal role in decision-making affairs and body of such village council is locally known as *bhaiyari*. In this regard there is no voice of the *gaon basua*.

They have their own parental spirit, known as *chutter raj* in their territory. The Baiga of this spirit is called as *raj baiga*. It is also reported that the parental spirit among them of eastern and western regions of Palamou district are *chedi raj* and *dootho raj* respectively. They consider each of these spirits as their *malik or malakini*. Each territorial unit inhabited by the particular section of the tribe has separate identity: in the northern region it is known as *ilaka*, in the western region it is known as *pragnat* and in the eastern region it is known as *jamara*.

The supreme deity among them is *Dharti Mai* (Earth Goddess). Most of their supernatural beliefs are associated with their surrounding ecological niche such as, they used to worship *bagh* (tiger) which is known as *baghaut*, for the appeasement of all jungle-dwelling animals who can cause harm to them. *Mua puja* is claimed to be the sole axis of all the religious beliefs and practices throughout their life; *budi mai* is another deity who ensures their welfare.

Birhor

The Birhor, a nomadic tribe, roams from one place to another in search of food. They temporarily camp near the forest where they live in *kumba* or leaf hut with their family and kinsmen along with their movable property like hunting and gathering implements and artifacts. They shift their camp as soon as it is noticed that near the camping place game, edible roots and tubers get scarce. They move to other areas where these are in abundance. Their territories are mainly in Ranchi, Gumla, Singhbhum and Hazaribagh districts of Chotanagpur plateau of Bihar. The present investigation was carried among Gumla district of Bihar. They are also located in some parts of Orissa, West Bengal and Madhya Pradesh which are adjacent to Chotanagpur plateau of Bihar. They numbered only 4,377 as per 1981 census in Bihar. Their physical features have been classed as Proto-Australoid. In Mundari Birhor means "a woodman". They claim that both they and the Kharwar are same group and are descended from the Sun.

Due to scarcity of food they move from one place to another in small bands. Their chief occupation is hunting and gathering, snaring monkeys, tracking hare, deer, and other small games, collection of rope fibers for making ropes for sale or barter, collection of honey and bee wax, etc. Their hunting season last from October to the beginning of monsoons in June. From June to September they are engaged in cultivation. A section among them also practise incipient form of agriculture and slash and burn cultivation but majority are landless and live mainly by hunting and selling ropes. They also actively participated in weekly market where they sell their collected forest produce in lieu of salt.

The whole community may be divided into two, basing on their nature of movement, namely, the *uthlus* (the wanderer) and the *jaghis* or *thanias* (the settlers). A few Birhor (*jaghi*) have settled permanently and are engaged in cultivation but majority among them are landless and maintain their livelihood by hunting and selling bark ropes.

A Birhor settlement is known as *tanda* consisting of nearly half a dozen of small huts. The huts are of conical shape made of branches and leaves. Each family has one hut partitioned into two halves, viz., one serving as a storeroom and the other is kitchen-cum-sleeping room. Their material possession consists of iron axes, hunting nets of monkey, rope-making tools, etc., a few earthern pitchers, palm-leaf mats, wooden mortar and pestles, etc. It is reported that some *tandas* construct a small hut for their spirit *bongas* where tutelary clan deity is represented by pieces of stone and wooden pegs, etc. In some sites of *jagi* settlement area there is a sacred grove called *jily-jiyar*. This is the seat of the hunting spirits or *sendrabonga*.

Birhors are divided into number of exogamous totemistic clans, such as *murmu, bhaghwar, nankari, induar, ain, kachhua*, etc. Descent is traced through male line and marriage between same clan is forbidden.

The unstable subsistence pattern has forced them to shun any tribal in-group sentiment or cohesion among members of different clans. Members of the scattered group of families of a particular clan never come together as units in one clan organisation. However, occasionally, the members of the same clan who live in close proximity, attend the periodical clan ceremonies, when sacrifices are offered to the clan deities such as *Ora-bonga* or *Buru-bonga*. It is observed that in a *tanda* with families belonging to different clans appear to have a comparatively greater in-group feeling and unity than different families of the same clan but belonging to different *tanda*. *Tanda* membership, therefore, bind them with a bond of fraternity.

A *tanda* is composed of 8 to 12 families belonging to different clans who move about in band in search of food. Each of such groups has a headman—*naya*, who functions both as a priest and a secular headman. He is chosen by the gurdian spirit of a *tanda* and he alone can propitiate them and keep them in order and thereby can avert all odds and secure good luck for the *tanda* members. It is believed by their gurdian spirits that son of a deceased *naya* would be the next *naya* of the same *tanda*. Infact, *tanda* among Birhor is a kind of food quest group; this is not a kin-oriented group.

A Birhor's idea of life continuously progresses from stage to stage. At each successive stage, in their rites of passage, they are meant to protect themselves from the evil influences. After birth, mother and child are considered impure for 21 days and that is why they remain in a state of taboo. During the first seven days, the whole *tanda* observes pollution. Adult marriage through negotiation is customary rule but they also acquire their mate by *golat* (marriage by exchange), *duku* (marriage by intrusion), *ghar-damada* (keeping son-in-law), *devar-bhouji* (junior levirate) and *salibiya* (junior sororate). Marriage is solemnized with the help of their *pahan* (priest) and elderly members. During field investigation, we came to know that marriage rituals are taking place at bridegroom's residence where bride comes from her residence. Vermilion application on the forehead of a bride is the prime ritual of their marriage. They bury their dead in their own burial ground. The pollution period lasts for ten days but on third day, that is, on *tihi* lineage members perform *mundan* (saving of head hair) and on the tenth day *gami* are held where community as well as *tanda* members are fed. Birhors believe that death is caused by some malevolent spirit. They also believe that dead man's soul need not always be reborn in his own community.

Since they live in forest environment, their whole belief system is centered around the local ecosystem. "All his religious rites and rituals have for their object the propitiation and conciliation of these supernatural powers of various grades of potency and sanctity, with a view to secure luck and to avoid misfortune and to prevent disease and dearth of food, etc." (Prasad, 1961). In their religious beliefs they are surrounded by supernatural beings and spirits. Thus, they try to force themselves from trouble by spell and threat and other types of magic.

Asur

Asurs are believed to be the direct descendants of the ancient people of that name who were associated with the art of working on metals and who were the makers of the various metal relics discovered in the Asur sites in Chotanagpur (Leuva, 1963). Bir-Asur is synonymous for them. Asur—the iron-smelter—is one of the primitive tribal groups in Bihar.

According to Risley (1981, reprinted), Asur is a small non-Aryan tribe who lives almost entirely by iron-smelting. According to S.C. Roy (1926) Asurs are divided into some sections based on occupational involvement, namely: (a) Soika Asurs, also known as Agarias, who live in jungle and hills and smelt iron, (b) Bir Asur or Birjias, living in forest and hilly clad area practising iron-smeltering and basket-weaving, and (c) Jait Asur mostly living in villages and making iron implements. Some of the sections have taken up agriculture as one of their profession.

The Asurs are confined in Bihar and Madhya Pradesh. The present investigation is carried out in Chotanagpur plateau of Bihar region where they are confined in Palamau, Gumla and Lohardaga districts. It is reported that under Bishunpur police station of Gumla district, their concentration is maximum mainly around the villages of Jovipat, Polpolpat. They are also found in police stations of Ghaghra, Chainpur, Latehar, Lohardaga and Mahuadanr. As per 1981 census, they numbered 7,783. The Asur inhabit in the 'Pat' (table land on the hill) area of Netarhat plateau of Bihar. This tract of their homeland is full of forests, hills and small table lands.

Traditionally, the Asur were iron-smelters and *beonra* (slash and burn) cultivators. They have now become primarily agriculturists. Besides, hunting and collection of roots, fruits and flowers constitute the additional economic pursuits. Hunting is more of relaxation and pastime than one of the regular economic activities. Presently, iron smelting is not lucrative as well as scarcity in raw materials and hence they are unable to maintain their family. Therefore, they are forced to switch over to various gainful economic pursuits of which wage labour in bauxite mine is considered to be lucrative. A few among them are service-holders. It is observed that they prefer to settle in the form of village at sufficiently high table land because land erosion will be less in monsoon and, therefore, they would get enough *bari* (kitchen garden) land for their maize cultivation. It is also reported that many among them in the past migrated to tea gardens of north Bengal and Assam and as wage labour to Andaman Island.

They are divided into a number of exogamous totemistic *gotra* or clan, namely, *mendhak* (frog), *aiyen* (a fish), *minj* (a fish), etc. The chief function of the clans is to regulate marital alliances, violation of which, is believed to bring misfortune. They form an endogamous group and practise clan exogamy. Now-a-days adult marriage is prevalent. Monogamy is the rule. The second wife is not usually taken so long as the first is alive and is not barren. Remarriage is allowed. Marriage is solemnised with the help of *pahan* of their own. They also acquire their mate through *gharjamai*, exchange of sister or *golat*, junior levirate or *devar-bhouji biya*, junior sororate or *sali biya* and marriage by elopement or *duku*, etc. Marriage by negotiation or *sadhi* is the common form of acquiring mate. System of bride-price or *dalipaisa* is prevalent among them. Formerly, a pig used to be an essential item of the bride-price. But in case the bridegroom is not in a position to pay the bride-price immediately, the bride accompanies him and the formal marriage ceremony is postponed till suitable time and day. Divorce is allowed but not encouraged. Divorce proceeding is held before panchayat and the rate of divorce is getting accelerated in their close society too perhaps due to they intrusion of cash which they earn from bauxite mine as wage earner. Divorce compensation is also given to either party. After divorce, usually the children stay with their biological father. The existence of youth dormitory or *dhumkuria* is now becoming a legend among them but *akhara* (open dancing ground) still exists in many villages. Birth in a family brings pollution of *chhut* for nine days. The delivery takes place in the house where midwife or *dai or kushrayan* of their own community attends.

Disposal of dead through burial is common. All the belongings of the deceased are also buried. They have their own burial place; they must take bath after returning from burial ground. Pollution lasts for 10 days. Before burying the dead, they touch fire on the mouth of the deceased. On the tenth day, *kaman* is observed, that is, they shave their beard and cut their head hair by themselves and a community feast is held and thus their pollution period is over. They also observe the ritual of inviting the soul of the deceased which is locally known as *umbul ader*. It has been observed that usually their burial ground is situated near water-shed but far away from their hamlet.

They have their own *jati panchayat* which is headed by *mahata* or *mukhiya* and he is assisted by *pujar* or *pahan*. Usually the verdict of their panchayat is honoured and in case of any violation the defaulter or offender leaves the village forever. Generally, fines are imposed. The role and importance of their traditional panchayat has gradually weakened due to implementation of statutory *gram panchayat*.

The Asur believe in *singh-bonga, marang-bonga* and various other *bongas* which are known to their *pahan*. They also observed their traditional *sarhi kutasi* ritual for the prosperity of their iron-smelting work in which a chicken is sacrificed. This age-old ritual is still practised though many among them have left their traditional iron-smelting work. They also worship their ancestors. They believe in witchcraft, benevolent and malevolent spirits. *Mati* and *ojha*—witch doctors—are consulted during crisis period. Along with their traditional belief and practices, they also celebrate *sarhul, phagua, sohrai, karma* and *kharwaz* or *nawakhani* rituals with their neighbouring Hindu caste groups.

It is also found from the field observation that some among them have adopted Christianity and they are proud of their present way of life and consider themselves higher in status from their non-Christian brethren. The Christian Asur have also adopted modern agricultural techniques and among them education is becoming popular. Here also, immediate ecological niche and local natural resources have influenced not only their belief system but also their age-old occupation.

Korwa

The Korwa, a Kolarian tribe, affirm that they have seven endogamous divisions, viz., *Dhari, Sinduria, Paharia, Koraku, Agaria, Kheria/Tisia* and *Guyning Korwa*. Sandhwar (1972, unpublished) also reports the existence of these divisions among the Korwa. Usually, their territory is surrounded by forest. The present investigation has been carried out among Paharia Korwa or Hill Korwa of Gumla district of Bihar. Those who live in plains are known as Dharia Korwa. According to their folk tale, they have originated from the scarecrows set up by the first men of Sarguja to protect their crops from wild animals by frightening them away. The Korwa were born of those scarecrows after they were animated by the Supreme Being. They are distributed in Raigarh, Bilaspur and Sarguja district of Madhya Pradesh, in

Mahuadanr block of Palamou district and in Chainpur and Kurdeg block of Gumla district of Bihar. They numbered 21,940 in Bihar as per 1981 census. The literacy rate among them is 2.95 per cent in Bihar.

It has been observed that Hill Korwa villages are on the top of hills with a thick forest. Traditionally, they were *beonra* (slash and burn) cultivators, hunters and food-gatherers. Since *beonra* is banned any more, they have gradually become settled cultivators. As they have insufficient and unfertile land they cannot produce enough and so they cannot depend on agriculture for their livelihood throughout the year. In fact, they possess *tanr* (non-irrigated) type land on the hills and hill-slopes. Due to this, they mostly depend on wage labour in unorganised sector except during monsoon. They also make baskets and sell them in the weekly market. To substantiate their economy, they also practise hunting and involve themselves in the collection from forest products such as *sal* twig used as *datan, mahulain* leaves, *gethi* (a kind of edible tuber), *nakoa* (a kind of edible tuber), *koenar* leave, *phutkal* leave, *mahua* fruit, *char* (a fruit), *kendu* leaf and fruit and bamboo for their basketry. It has been observed that they barter *char* (Chiraunji—a fruit) for salt in the weekly market. They get 30 to 40 *paila* of salt in exchange of one *paila char* (it is reported that one *paila* measuring about 1,100 gm; *char* seed is a kind of dry fruit which costs around Rs.150 to Rs.180 per kg. in the market). Mahua is also exchanged for rice. Other things are sold in cash and with that money they purchase their necessary commodities. Their agricultural produce comprise rice, millet, maize and some vegetables for their consumption. Now-a-days, it is found that the Korwa in the studied area hardly can supplement their income from forest due to various restrictions.

They have totemic *killi* (clans) and for marriage they

practise clan exogamy. A clan is divided into *khili-bans* (lineage). The members of *khili-bans* partake of the same sacrificial food made from the head of a sacrificed goat, pig or chicken. It is not shared with the members of other *khili-bans*. A *khili-bans* is associated with the place of its origin which they call *baiga-asthan*. Most of them hold that their *baiga-asthan* is located in Sarguja District. In course of time, the members of a *khili-bans* moved away from their *baiga-asthan* and settled down at different places where it was easy for them to earn their livelihood. However, they find out their actual kinship relationships if they come to know that they have same *baiga-asthan*.

As per customary rule, the Korwa have to practise clan exogamy. But it is found that most of them have forgotten their clans. Hence, they practise *khili-bans* or lineage exogamy. They are usually monogamous. *Biya* (marriage by negotiation) is the rule. But *dhukadhuki* (love marriage), *gulat* (marriage by exchange), *dever biya* (junior levirate), *salibiya* (junior sororate), *ghar-de-jewa* (accommodating son-in-law in the house), etc., are also practised by them. Marriage by service and remarriage or *sagai* are also allowed. System of bride-price or *negi* or *dali-paisa* is prevalent among them. With the approval of their *jati panchayat*, divorce is allowed on the ground of extramarital affairs, barrenness, impotency, incurable diseases, laziness, etc. If a woman is divorced due to her extramarital relationship, then her husband demands Rs.40 to Rs.50 from wife's father or from the person who remarries her. Children stay with the father in case of divorce. They usually bury their dead; community members participate in their funeral procession. After ten or fifteen days *kaman* ritual takes place, when all the villagers irrespective of their caste or tribal affiliation are invited to participate in the feast. The soul of the deceased is believed to enter the body of a newly born baby in the house. On the day of *kaman*, five members of different *khili-bans* are offered cooked rice and pulses by the deceased person's family after purification. This custom is known as *panch kuanri*. It is believed that the soul of the deceased soul comes back to the house on that day. The souls of the ancestors are remembered during all the ceremonies and festivals when food offerings are made to them.

Ancestor worship is common among the Korwa tribe. They believe that their happiness, and miseries depend upon the will of their gods, goddesses and spirits. So, the deities and spirits are propitiated through the *baiga*—the village priest.

They believe that *Bhagwan* (Sun) is their supreme God. They believe that is the creator and protector of the universe. Apart from this, they also believe in *dhartimai* as a powerful goddess. They also have faith in number of malevolent spirits who are believed to trouble them and these spirits are also propitiated by offering goat, chicken, etc. They believe in witchcraft practices. The witch doctors help them to identify the spirit that cause disease or misery.

Didyai

Didyai—a primitive tribal group—is found in Kudumuluguma block of Malkangiri district of Orissa. The Didyai are scattered over 37 villages. This least known tribal group is confined to a stretch of about 35 kms between Duduma falls and the Kondakamberu range along the river Machkund of the district. In fact, this part of the tribal habitat is infested with thick forest, is less populated and is mostly inaccessible. According to information received from block office they numbered 4,470 as per 1993 block survey and total household was 1,138. Except 12 villages, all the 25 villages are inhabited by Didyai population. Demographic picture of Didyai villages is described through the following table:

	Name of the Village	Total no. of Households	M	F	Remarks
1.	Muduriguda (a)	87	162	183	Mixed Village
2.	Oringi	115	223	255	Do
3.	Purnaguma	29	67	71	Do
4.	Chilipadhar	18	36	21	Mixed Village
5.	Tikra Para (a)	34	69	76	-
6.	Tikra Para (b)	30	57	71	-
7.	Bia Para	28	57	62	-
8.	Suri Para	18	51	67	-
9.	Kaning	16	39	32	Mixed village
10.	Nira Pari	23	50	49	Do
11.	Ganga Para	63	130	110	-
12.	Khajuri guda	21	37	42	-
13.	Naringjhola	18	36	42	-
14.	Amblibeda	63	96	122	-
15.	Bodankia guda	64	92	112	-
16.	Dandvabeda	71	166	148	-
17.	Ghishing beda	53	105	93	-
18.	Angru guda	18	37	39	-
19.	Muduri guda (b)	6	11	11	Mixed village
20.	Bataguda	22	33	53	-
21.	Karkaguda	32	61	73	-
22.	Barlelubandha	15	32	36	-
23.	Bamrin	13	32	35	-
*24.	Orapadhar	59	107	102	Mixed village
*25.	Kante manjari	12	19	18	-
*26.	Araling Para	11	16	19	-
*27.	Taberu	38	71	60	-

Contd...

Contd...

*28.	Dabuguda	26	46	51	-
*29.	Totaguda	22	38	34	-
*30.	Mari beda	15	33	28	-
*31.	Ranguda	2	4	3	Mixed village
*32.	Jantri	16	21	22	Do
*33.	Kodigandhi	3	5	7	Do
*34.	Disariguda	9	17	22	-
*35.	Sanyasiguda	8	10	21	Mixed village
*36.	Dhakada padar	38	70	71	-
*37.	Nadimanjari	17	34	28	-

* All these 14 villages are isolated from the main land by Chitragunda reservoi: on which Balimela Hydel Power Project is established.

Didyai villages are usually found in hilly slopes. The village Biapara is located at an altitude of 3,500 feet above the sea level. Now-a-days, most of them are settled in the plain areas of this region. They were traditionally shifting hill-cultivators. Now they also have adopted settled plough cultivation. The houses of villages in the hill are more isolated than the houses in the plain. The Didyai speak a dialect which comes under non-Kherwari branch of Munda group in the Austro-Asiatic division of the Austric family. It is close to the dialect of Gadaba, Saora, Bondo, Juang and Kharia.

The livelihood of Didyai is chiefly dependent on gathering which is substantiated by, especially, shifting cultivation. Till date hunting and gathering has played a key role in their livelihood pattern. With the help of digging stick in the forest, they collect various edible roots, tubers, leaves, fruits and flowers which also vary seasonally. The palm-wine (salap) is very sweet and favourite drink among them. The mahua flower is one of the forest produce, collected by them during the season, that is, from end of February to Middle of

May. The mahua flower is not only consumed directly but it also helps in preparation of country-made liquor. Seeds of mahua are also collected for oil extraction; such oil is used for cooking and lighting the *diya* (lamp). During the season of *ulih* (mango), they consume it as a part of their diet and also gather the kernels of mango. During July-August, when there is tremendous monsoon, they usually suffer from insufficient food when they crush the collected kernels into powder and finally mix them in water to make it like a gruel and consume it.

Most favourite edible wild plant is tender bamboo shoots. Other roots and tubers collected by the Didyai, in this area, are *tamo* (dorkanda), *toria* (toraj kanda), *gbu* (bara kanda), *kirla* (pota kanda), *kondala* (pet kanda), etc. Apart from these, *gha*—a kind of root—is also collected from forest by them for consumption during summer and monsoon. *Tamo* is collected by them for consumption during February to May, while *torla* is collected during July to September, the *kondala* root is available to them during August to September and *kirla* is available during July to August. These are eaten after boiling. They also collect edible leaves neighbouring like *gudiali* during May and June, *bhaji, chadibade, dooli, korlaha*, etc., from their forest during rainy season. Apart from all these, *chatni* of red ant or *hione* is consumed throughout the year which they collect from the forest and make it into paste after grinding and adding salt, chilly and tamarind. *Bidi* leaves—*kendu*, are collected from the forest for their own consumption. Some of them sell *kendu* leaves in the weekly market for hard cash, to meet other household expenses.

Once hunting was an important economic pursuit among the Didyai. But, at present, wild games are scarce and moreover Forest Act has been imposed, which restricts them from hunting. But they practise hunting secretly in the neighbouring forest area. With the help of bow and arrow they hunt hare, birds and squirrel. It is reported that they are good archers. Before going for hunt they pray to their jungle deity (*bangur*) for the success of their expedition. But they strictly avoid the flesh of tiger, snake and bear because these are tabooed to them. Fishing is also done by them; during summer after poisoning the pool of water by a fruit—*ponoralasia,* which is available from their immediate forest. Apart from this, hand-nets and fishing-baskets like *gungur, dandar,* etc., are also used.

Till today, *bri* or *podu* (shifting cultivation) is practised by them on the hill-slope villages of Didyai land. The principal means of livelihood centres around *bri* which is substantiated by settled plough cultivation. It is observed that a Didyai family always prefers his *bri* land near to his village. In such a *bri* land, crops produced by them are: *dahua* (a kind of millet), *dira* (Panicum italicum), *hua* (Pancium miliare), *romia* (black gram), *give* (red gram), etc. Rotation of crops is practised by them. In the first year, the seeds of *dira,* black gram, red gram, brinjal, tomato are broadcasted in a single *bri* plot. In the second year, *hua* (Panicum miliare) is produced from the same piece of plot and in the third year, *dehua* (a kind of millet) is sown and after that the said plot is abandoned for a couple of years. On the contrary, the foothill-Didyai adopted settled cultivation along with *bri* cultivation. This (plough cultivation) is gaining importance in their economic life.

It is observed from Oringi village and Tumbapadar hamlet that they still exchange their forest produce and grain against their essential domestic articles at weekly market at Kudumuluguma or Mundiguda. Induction of cash economy is recent one. Through cash they buy dress, cattle, utensils and ornaments of women for their personal adornments.

The Didyai are endogamous having two exogamous divisions or moietieo. The person who hails from one group is called *nairamoan* (the group of brothers) while the other group from which marriage partners are selected called *moita* (the group of friends). Marriage is tabooed within the same division.

Every half, i.e., each exogamous division is having five totemic groups, viz., *gbe* (bear), *nkoo* (tiger), *mala* (cobra), *goi* (tortoise), and *misali* (crocodile). Again each such totemic groups is having group of clans except tortoise and crocodile totemic groups. The groups of clans with a common totem is known as *gta* (lineage), which are exogamous and a number of *gtas* form one large exogamous division of dual organisation.

Their families are small, monogamy is prevalent. Normally, negotiation marriage (*toso*) is encouraged though *udalia* (marriage by capture) and *gariye* (marriage by service) are also practised. Bride-price (*gneng*) system is present among them. Delivery of a child takes place in corner of the living room which is attended by senior women preferably of the same lineage. After birth, the navel cord is cut by an arrow incase of male issue while for female issue it is cut with a knife. The placenta and other things are wrapped with some leaves and buried in the corner of the house, to protect the baby from evil eye. Iron bangles are put on the baby after six days, to protect him/her from evil eye. Didyais think that death occurs only during old age. Apart from this, death may also be caused by some malevolent spirit. They usually cremate the corpse except in the case of death of small child, pregnant woman and death due to cholera, small pox, etc., in which they bury the dead. There are a series of rituals for cremation or burial and observance of pollution period; all these are practised to please the departed soul as well as the ancestor souls; otherwise malevolent spirits will harm them.

From these beliefs and practices of Didyai, it is observed that there is enough influence of natural environment on their religious pantheon. It is reported that mother goddess is worshipped as the Supreme Being ' and fertility cult is practised in principle (Guha et al, 1968). Contextual observation reflects that Didyai month starts from new moon and they practise the following rituals which are closely connected with their ecosystem. Goesendia—the God of hill where they go for hunting, Ghia Pande is worshipped in view of first fruit ceremony, ritual hunting, welfare of children and cattle, and to propitiate the supreme deity of forest and spirits of dead animals while they proceed for hunting. During monsoon in the month of June-July they perform osarke pande, which is regarded as sowing ceremony. To protect their agricultural land from evil eye and wild animals who usually destroy their crop fields, they perform golota ritual in the months of October-November. During the months of December-January they celebrate pusarke pande which is represented by eating of first peas and worship of their cattle and mother earth whose blessings give them sufficient yield of sweet peas. The first monsoon is welcomed by them with a ritual called sanraik hai. If god Bokpa is pleased they get sufficient quantity of salap (palm-wine). Ancestors' spirits and souls are worshipped in every month under big and old tree of the village. The hunters worship bangur—the forest deity —for favour. They also worship mountain God—Jiramolu.

There are a series of beliefs in magical practices in Didyai society. For Example, when a child cries without any sufficient reason, then benevolent ancestral spirits are invoked for help while, when a child gets illness, the malevolent spirits are propitiated. They use of herbal medicine in case of their ailments, e.g., hiansla (tangani seali) fruit is used for treatment of colic pain.

The above discussion clearly speaks of their close interaction with forest environment.

Abuj Maria

The Abuj Maria or Abujh Maria, a lesser known tribal community live in the Abuj Marh hill tract of Madhya Pradesh. Etymologically, the word 'Abuj Marh' or 'Abujh Marh' means unknown hills and thus the people of the area are Abujh or Abuj Maria. The name Abuj Maria has probably been given to them by the outsiders. They generally introduce or prefer to introduce themselves as Meta Koitor. Here 'Meta' means hills and the term 'Koitor' is used by all the Gond people as their generic name. Generally, the Koitor are of two types—the Meta Koitor and the Dor Koitor. Those who live in the hilly tract or *meta bhum* are Meta Koitor and those live in the plains or low land are Dor Koitor. As the Abuj Maria live in the hilly tracts, they are Meta Koitor. The Abuj Marh hills are situated in the north-western part of Bastar district of Madhya Pradesh. Bastar district is the largest district of Madhya Pradesh with a total area of 39,114 sq kms with maximum number of tribal population; 72 per cent of the total population of the district are of tribal origin. The Abuj Marh area of the district is an extensive hilly terrain of 3,900 kms. It is bounded by Antagarh tehsil in the north which is a plain land. On the south of the hills there is Indrawati river, on the east the Narayanpur tehsil and on the west the hilly tract is bounded by Kotri river. The Abuj Maria are distributed in 236 villages, of which 189 villages are under Narayanpur tehsil, 39 villages under Bijapur tehsil, 8 villages are under Dantewada tehsil and they number 19,250 as per 1981 census. Village-wise demographic account is given below:

Village-wise Demography of Abuj Maria (1981 census)

Tehsil	Name of the Village	Total Population of the Village			Abuj Maria		Other (SC/ST)	
		M	F	Total	M	F	M	F
A. Narayanpur Tehsil								
1.	Kodhur	37	30	67	37	30		
2.	Tekameta	17	19	36	17	19		
3.	Mangebeda (Musfarsi)	8	5	13	8	5		
4.	Kathor	14	14	28	14	14		
5.	Pareyadi	12	14	26	12	14		
6.	Orchapar	9	10	19	9	10		
7.	Kumchal	Deserted						
8.	Palemeta	Deserted						
9.	Kongoli	28	27	55	28	27		
10.	Gamandli	27	33	60	27	33		
11.	Hikonar	26	20	46	26	20		
12.	Kader	9	10	19	9	10		
13.	Gumchur	26	27	53	26	27		
14.	Turko	34	38	72	34	38		
15.	Tumeradi	32	28	60	32	28		
16.	Bherabeda	Deserted						
17.	Maskur	58	49	107	57	49	1	
18.	Hiranginar	19	14	33	19	14		
19.	Horadi	32	32	64	32	32		
20.	Kanchchapal	49	46	95	49	46		
21.	Kanagaon	73	68	141	69	63	4	5
22.	Garawahi	21	17	38	21	17		
23.	Guner	8	10	18	8	10		
24.	Toke	51	64	115	51	64		
25.	Markur	6	6	12	6	6		

Contd...

Contd...

26.	Sargipal	36	36	72	36	36		
27.	Palahur	13	9	22	13	9		
28.	Kundla	60	61	121	60	61		
29.	Jetwar	30	31	61	30	31		
30.	Vogan	20	25	45	20	25		
31.	Tarobeda	20	24	44	20	24		
32.	Maspi	20	14	34	20	14		
33.	Gomeh	58	56	114	57	56	1	
34.	Adnar	101	99	200	101	99		
35.	Malmeta	61	57	118	61	57		
36.	Vellar	13	21	34	13	21		
37.	Rawanadi	4	5	9	4	5		
38.	Hamokal	33	40	73	33	40		
39.	Marsulnapa	47	41	88	45	38	2	3
40.	Tarogonda	18	18	36	18	18		
41.	Chotebarekot	16	20	36	16	20		
42.	Konjey	44	47	91	44	47		
43.	Darangar	11	11	22	11	11		
44.	Kormokoro	26	23	49	26	23		
45.	Koroskoro	Destered						
46.	Ranimarke	24	34	58	24	34		
47.	Koronar	29	32	61	29	32		
48.	Kongey	49	51	100	48	51	1	
49.	Kangur	41	32	73	41	32		
50.	Jharawahi	21	19	40	21	19		
51.	Bornirpi	19	17	36	19	17		
52.	Kurusnar (Belmori)	Destered						
53.	Hechekuti	17	22	39	17	22		
54.	Binagunda	28	35	63	28	35		
55.	Garpa	21	27	48	18	22	3	
56.	Markabera	16	17	33	16	17		
57.	Warapenda	40	34	74	40	34		

Contd...

Contd...

No.	Name							
58.	Tahakadond	49	41	90	49	41		
59.	Motechnadi	16	19	35	16	19		
60.	Goredapadar (Korenar)	Destered						
61.	Bondom	Destered						
62.	Karkabera	24	17	41	24	17		
63.	Palahur	26	33	59	26	33		
64.	Dhuma	Deserted						
65.	Ousebeda	43	32	75	43	32		
66.	Kasturmeta	47	51	98	41	43	6	5
67.	Padamkot	52	60	112	52	60		
68.	Burungmar (Kodenar)	Deserted						
69.	Oksmarka	Deserted						
70.	Kutul	144	131	275	132	110	12	21
71.	Nelangur	53	47	100	53	47		
72.	Kumnar	9	7	16	9	7		
73.	Alnar	10	10	20	10	10		
74.	Ahenar	33	31	64	33	31		
75.	Kokameta	355	369	724	274	287	12	14
	(It is a mixed village of other tribal group like Bison Horn Maria or Dandani Maria)							
76.	Korenar	13	17	30	11	13	2	4
77.	Wasing	39	38	77	22	17	17	21
78.	Gongla	15	19	34	15	19		
79.	Becha	48	43	91	36	34	12	9
80.	Murnar	70	72	142	69	71	1	1
81.	Orchakorai	10	8	18	10	8		
82.	Irkbhatti	88	99	187	88	99		
83.	Irpanar	18	25	43	18	25		
84.	Jharawahi	109	111	220	101	104	8	7
85.	Dhunta	43	57	100	36	49	7	8
86.	Haltanar	74	71	145	74	71		
87.	Garmunjur	2	2	4	2	2		

Contd...

Contd...

88.	Mahakanar	5	3	8	5	3	
89.	Dondribera	7	9	16	7	9	
90.	Orcha	227	204	431	188	172	
91.	Gudari	100	93	193	100	93	
92.	Markabera	45	34	79	45	34	
93.	Juwara	151	137	288	149	131	
94.	Kodkanar	34	26	60	-	-	34 26
95.	Taronar	18	14	32	14	11	
96.	Taranar (Gardebera)	9	4	13	6	1	
97.	Nednar	48	33	81	48	33	
98.	Nerameta (Bipdiya)	29	37	66	26	32	
99.	Hikpar	24	32	56	15	19	
100.	Okpar (Brehabera)	46	32	78	31	24	
101.	Torokur (Badur)	14	19	33	14	19	
102.	Mohandi	17	16	33	17	16	
103.	Kodoli	13	15	28	13	15	
104.	Kurusnar (Khargaon)	60	64	124	59	64	
105.	Geulapadar	24	38	62	24	38	
106.	Kumnar	24	25	49	24	25	
107.	Kornar (Ghoragaon)	15	12	27	15	12	
108.	Kandari	63	65	128	63	65	
109.	Alwar	21	17	38	21	17	
110.	Gumiapal (Munjbera)	Deserted					
111.	Kodeliar	60	65	125	60	65	
112.	Kornar	49	42	91	49	42	
113.	Ghattakal	36	50	86	36	50	
114.	Gurdai	88	103	191	88	103	
115.	Dumnar	24	25	49	24	25	
116.	Gunter (Wayenger)	19	14	33	19	14	
117.	Moksanli	62	55	117	62	55	
118.	Asnar	90	95	185	89	95	1 -
119.	Rainar (Bhatbeda)	69	63	132	69	63	

Contd...

Contd...

120.	Mandali	41	39	80	41	39
121.	Konda Koti	19	31	50	19	31
122.	Harbel	72	68	140	72	68
123.	Donderbera	87	81	168	87	81
124.	Ader	95	102	197	95	102
125.	Kudmel	168	154	322	168	154
126.	Kalmanar	44	45	89	42	44
127.	Kutulnar	50	52	102	46	47
128.	Karkanar	39	39	78	39	39
129.	Kotenar	28	24	52	26	23
130.	Kangali	32	40	72	32	40
131.	Acheli	Deserted				
132.	Irpanar	Deserted				
133.	Adimpar	23	27	50	23	27
134.	Kahakori	14	16	30	14	16
135.	Khodpar	35	44	79	35	44
136.	Gumarka	99	87	186	99	87
137.	Dhurbeda	47	49	96	47	49
138.	Rashbeda	57	52	109	57	50
139.	Mathbeda	65	51	116	65	51
140.	Michebeda	26	21	47	26	21
141.	Gattakal	46	56	102	46	56
142.	Dhoubey	62	68	130	62	68
143.	Metabeda	37	28	65	37	28
144.	Koyamata	55	59	114	55	59
145.	Kortamarka	42	39	81	42	39
146.	Nelnar	75	77	152	75	77
147.	Kostari	5	5	10	5	5
148.	Gomagal	89	77	166	89	77
149.	Kokapar	46	49	95	46	49
150.	Chalcher	133	158	291	(All are Dandami Maria).	
151.	Idnar	14	22	36	14	22

Contd...

Contd...

152.	Barehtondabeda	53	59	112	53	59
153.	Chotetondabeda	38	38	76	38	38
154.	Jabgonda	130	124	254	(All are Dandami Maria).	
155.	Koduli	85	85	170	(All are Dandami Maria).	
156.	Bhotia	19	17	36	19	17
157.	Tonindogra	29	39	68	29	39
158.	Katurbeda	30	35	65	21	29
159.	Hitulwar	26	29	55	23	26
160.	Barehberkot	16	21	37	16	21
161.	Brehbeda	32	32	64	32	32
162.	Motentoda	28	23	51	28	23
163.	Metanar (Matahanar)	21	20	41	21	20
164.	Botor	6	4	10	6	4
165.	Gandawar	14	11	25	14	11
166.	Godelmarka	20	20	40	20	20
167.	Gumaradi (Gomadhari)	19	29	48	19	29
168.	Balehbeda (Balehmeta)	21	26	47	21	26
169.	Murhapadar	26	34	60	20	25
170.	Khorehpar	Deserted				
171.	Garbeda (Harimarka)	3	2	5	3	2
172.	Moyanteleh	16	11	27	16	11
173.	Palehmeta	Deserted				
174.	Neskar	Deserted				
175.	Chindpur	11	17	28	11	17
176.	Orchameta	67	69	136	66	69
177.	Bhangobheriya	Deserted				
178.	Majhi Khutni	31	29	60	21	29
179.	Khelahbeda	Deserted				
180.	Nariya	Deserted				
181.	Kotoli	6	5	11	5	4
182.	Huchacha Kot	47	3,4	81	33	25
183.	Koburhur	6	9	15	6	9

Contd...

Contd...

184.	Hikmeta	5	11	16	5	11
185.	Musparsi	46	25	71	41	17
186.	Krohogerah	17	24	41	17	24
187.	Korchgaon	29	19	47	29	19
188.	Harimarka	2	1	3	2	1
189.	Rengabeda	6	3	9	6	3

B. Bijapur Tehsil

190.	Jatlur	145	123	268	126	122
191.	Diwalur	53	36	89	53	36
192.	Padmeta	34	42	76	34	42
193.	Dodimarka	51	42	93	51	42
194.	Boter	46	42	88	46	42
195.	Talwara	16	12	28	16	12
196.	Karangul	50	54	104	50	54
197.	Murumwade	91	78	169	91	78
198.	Gundehkot	23	19	42	23	19
199.	Lanka	82	94	176	(Fully Dandami Maria Village)
200.	Rekawaya	29	21	50	29	21
201.	Tahakawada	24	26	50	24	26
202.	Lekhwada	62	58	120	62	58
203.	Adesmeta	87	84	171	87	84
204.	Komhu	51	49	100	51	49
205.	Behlar	Deserted
206.	Ponchawada	44	57	101	44	57
207.	Korowaya	6	8	14	6	8
208.	Hitul	236	250	486	231	248
209.	Khalhaza	33	30	63	33	30
210.	Alwada	30	25	55	30	25
211.	Pindiyakot	312	294	606	242	231
212.	Ghot	23	29	52	23	29
213.	Duseli	Deserted.

Contd...

Contd...

214.	Dunge	487	425	912	475	411
215.	Betehkal	30	28	58	30	28
216.	Rotar	69	55	124	69	55
217.	Ringabeda	Deserted				
218.	Aderh	Deserted				
219.	Nendurkurch	41	42	83	41	42
220.	Bhatbeda	10	3	13	10	3
221.	Tarnar	30	28	58	30	28
222.	Otanghi	Deserted				
223.	Mungari	17	22	39	17	22
224.	Gawari	4	4	8	4	4
225.	Modambade	27	24	51	27	24
226.	Mohonar	17	17	34	17	17
227.	Kuyeh	28	23	51	28	23
228.	Thultuli	112	126	238	112	126
C. Dantewada Tehsil						
229.	Hikul	99	96	195	99	96
230.	Pindekapal	49	70	119	49	70
231.	Toyenar	115	125	240	115	125
232.	Paralnar	61	62	123	61	62
233.	Tahkawada	41	42	83	41	42
234.	Kodokal	25	25	50	25	25
235.	Handawade	227	209	436	203	186
236.	Hitawada	297	279	576	293	275
	(Total Abuj Maria 19,250 souls as per 1981 census)					

Abuj Marh area is covered extensively with hills and hillocks, with streams and dense forest. Abuj Maria culture is nourished within the undisturbed ecosystem. The area is very isolated, ill-communicated and is also declared as restricted area by the state government. It is reported that they belong to Proto-Australoid group and their dialect is under

Dravidian family. They speak Gondi.

Traditionally, the people are *penda* (slash-and-burn or shifting hill) cultivators. As they inhabit the hilly terrain full of jungle, *penda* is the most suitable and easy process of cultivation. Till date they have been practising *penda* as their primary source of earning. They produce various types of cereals and millets such as *kolha*, *kosra* etc. Along with *penda*, now-a-days, they are engaged in settled plough cultivation. Even then, *penda* is the most preferred type of cultivation. Rice is the chief crop from plough cultivation. As they live in the forest surrounding, they get plenty of forest products which are very important in their day-to-day life. Mahua is an important item grown abundantly in their locality. Mahua tree is important in their life and culture. They collect the flower for their own consumption. They prepare some sweet dish from this flower. They also extract liquor from the flower which is an essential item in their lifecycle rituals, in all their religious festivals and in all formal and informal gatherings. It is believed that their ancestors and deities are never satisfied without receiving the offering of mahua liquor. The excess quantity of this flower is either stored for future use, or sold or exchanged with cereals and pulses if it is required. They are not allowed to eat any new mahua flower without performing its ritual—*Irpu Pandum*. The seed of mahua flower, locally known as *dori* or *tora* is also a valuable item to them. They use it as cooking medium, to lit lamp and also to massage the body and head. Next to mahua, mango is another important item grown in their locality and in surrounding jungles. It is one of their chief food item used in their cooking. Similar words are also to be mentioned about the tamarind. All these three items grow both in their locality and also in the surrounding jungles. Except these, there are plenty of other food items they collect from jungle. They collect various types of roots, fruits, tubers, shoots, flowers, seeds, honey, leaves, leafy vegetables for cash earning. They get seasonal tasty items from the forest such as *putu* or mushroom, *basta* or young bamboo shoot, etc. They generally sell tamarind and *phooljharu* (locally available broom stick) for earning cash by which they purchase salt, clothes and other essential items.

Salfi or sulphi is a favourite juice. It is told that right from birth till death mahua liquor, and sulfi juice have special importance. After completion of pollution period, both after birth and death, mahua liquor is important to feed the relatives and friends. In marriages also the guests are entertained with liquor, *pej* and *landa*. It is observed that in their locality salfi trees grow in abundance and automatically their addiction towards salfi juice can not be ignored. Side by side, they have got some palm trees in their vicinity but they are less in number and they do not have any attraction towards its juice. Whereas in the Dorla belt of south Bastar, the palm trees grow in abundance and salfi grows in lesser number in comparison with palm tree. Palm tree and its juice have special importance in the life and culture of the Dorla. Their addiction towards palm juice is similar to the addiction of salfi juice of Abuj Maria people. Therefore, natural environment has a dominant role in determining the norms, customs and the behaviour pattern of the people of an area.

Traditionally, hunting was regarded as one of their subsidiary occupation. Gradually, due to implementation of Forest Act, restriction on hunting is imposed and side-by-side the number of animals in the jungle became less day-by-day. As a result, it is not possible to take hunting as an occupation. It lost its importance and at presently it is done only on some occasions specially on rituals and festivals. In their material culture, too, influence of forest is observed. They construct their houses with the sal logs, twigs, bamboo and grass which are all collected from forest. Among their household utensils leaf plates, cups and bowls are very common. Their cots, mats, baskets, bow, arrow, fishing trap, net and almost everything is prepared by the materials which are available in their forest.

The community is endogamous with a number of exogamous phratries. Each of the phratry has some smaller groups or clans locally known as *katta*. The *kattas* of each phratry is *dadabhai* or *saga* (consanguineal kins) with each other with a *bhaiband* tie. They are prohibited to have any marital relationship with a person of brother clan. Marriage can be soleminised in the *kattas* of other phratries which are known as wife's clan, i.e., *akomama* (*ako* means mother's and *mama* means brother). Their clans are named after some animals, fruits, flowers, birds, fishes, generally available in their locality. Each of the clan has its own deity locally known as *pen*. They worship their *pens* and trace their descent from their respective *pens*. Furthermore, in their celestial world the *pen* deities are again having genealogical relations; marriage within *dadabhai* relations of *pen* deity is tabooed. Descent is traced through father. They are patripotestal. Among them monogamy is the rule, polygyny is also allowed. They prefer to practise cross-cousing marriage. Generally, they prefer to arrange marriage from a nearby village due to physical inaccessibility or difficulty to travel to a long distance. Another reason for the preference of cross-cousin marriage (or *dudh lotana*) is due to bride-price system. In cross-cousin marriage one has to return the bride-price which is taken by him in his marriage. Automatically, the bride-price becomes less. *Pendul* or marriage by negotiation is the rule but love marriages are also not uncommon. They also practise *lamareh* (marriage by service), *aeohundi* (junior levirate), *vitte* (marriage by elopment), *koheberdan* (marriage by exchange), *koyeyari* (junior sororate), widow marriage, etc. Divorce is allowed but not encouraged in the society.

They have *ghotul* or youth dormitory of their own. It is completely of different type than the Muria *ghotul*. Their *ghotul* is open *ghotul*. It has no door. Among the Muria, the *ghotul* is closed. *Ghotul* is an institution, where the young boys and girls are taught about their customary laws and behaviour. In their *ghotul*, the boys and girls gather in the evening, sing, dance till late night, discuss about various village matters and then the girls come back to their homes. *Ghotul* also serves as a meeting place of the village elders. In a *ghotul*, they have *thanagudi* or a resting place for the outsiders. As they live in the forest clad villages, they are unable to travel during night. When they have to go to a distant place, they generally halt at a village during night and due to this reason in each and every village they have *thanagudi* or resting place for such travellers.

They believe that pregnancy occurs as per the wishes of heavenly father. As they live in the forest clad villages, they always have fear of unknown malevolent spirits. Due to this during pregnancy a woman generally avoids to go to the forest alone. Childbirth in a forest is regarded very bad as evil-eyes are there to harm the newly born baby and its mother. Pollution period lasts till the detachment of dried up umbilical cord from the body. In naming the child, they prefer to keep the name of their deceased ancestors. They have belief in rebirth. They always believe that their dead ancestors take birth in the family. Due to this they first notice if there is any birth mark or not. If there is any such mark they try to relate it with a member of their deceased relatives. In naming, they put a branch of a *tendu* tree in the child's hand, and begin to tell the names of their deceased friends and ancestors. When the branch falls down from the hand of the child they keep that name for the child. Among them, marriage takes place at the bridegroom's house. Pouring of oil, turmeric and water on the bride and bridegroom's head by the bridegroom's younger brother is the most important ritual.

They know that death takes place definitely due to some evil act of some evil spirit or due to magical performance by some person. They take the help of sorcerer to identify the actual cause of a death. Death pollution period continues for three days. They bury their dead. They have their traditional *jati panchayat*. The headman is known as *manjhi*. His post is hereditary. Abuj Marh area is divided into parganas and each pargana has several villages. In a pargana, there is a headman called as *pargana manjhi*. He heads over all the village *manjhis*. The *pargana panchayat* is the supreme political institution among them. Now-a-days, these parganas and their headmen have no real function. At present, they depend primarily on the statutory political organisation.

To adjust with their natural environment, automatically their life has adopted various measures which have penetrated into their culture. Habitation in an uncertain environment creates a feeling of helplessness in their mind. To overcome such a feeling they have taken support of the supreme authority in his various forms, very much adjusting with their natural environment. The deities live in jungle, in hills, rivers, streams, in winds and even in some trees. Sun is believed as the supreme authority, moon is his wife and the stars are their children. Sun gives light and warmth to the earth which ultimately created life on the earth. So he is regarded as supreme authority. *Tallur Muttey* is their mother goddess. She is the deity of their *bhum* or land. As they get their food from land, the *bhum* is regarded as their mother and she is recognised as *Tallur Muttey*. Among their other deities their ancestors and *pens* are also highly regarded. After the death of a person his or her soul is taken back to their own houses and established in the separate chamber known as *hanal katla*. Their ancestors are always thought as their protectors. On each and every ritual and festival, they must give special offerings to their ancestors. Their ancestors and *pens* are worshipped before starting of cultivation and after harvest. On the new rice eating ceremony they are first offered the newly harvested crops and cereals. Similarly, in case of season's first fruit eating ceremonies of mahua and mango, they first offer those to their ancestors and *pens*. Their *pens* have very important position in their life. They control the whole group of people and their society by their religious orders. Sometimes, they order through dreams, sometimes through possessions, etc. Their *pens* are genealogically related. Among their *pen* deities *Anga Deo, Deven Dokra, Paika Deo, Budha Deo, Raja Dokra*, etc., are very important. *Kaksar* is their chief festival performed in the month of June just before monsoon. It is the annual worship when all the clan deities, *Tallur Muttey*, and other deities including *Danteswari Mata* are worshipped. It is a festival through which they offer thanks to their clan deities and other deities after harvest of *urad* (Phaseclus radiatus). They are allowed to take it, only after offering it to the clan deities and their ancestors. They have a belief that if they have any new thing such as flowers, fruits, cereals and grains, if they do not offer it to their deities, they may face any type of danger specially the attack of tigers.

The seat of clan god is known as *pen-rawar*. It is a special shed under some big tree where they are not allowed to cut any tree. They are not allowed to cut many other trees for various social, economic and religious reasons. In this way, conservation of their local forest is maintained.

They have a vast knowledge of the medicinal plants

available in the vicinity. They are very much reluctant to go to the hospitals and health centres and instead they depend on their local forest resources. They generally do not destroy those plants also.

Dorla

The Dorla are distributed at the juncture of three states—Orissa, Andhra Pradesh and Madhya Pradesh. In Madhya Pradesh, they are found in the southern and south-western parts of Bastar district which meets in the east at the Malkangiri area of Orissa and in the west Khammam district of Andhra Pradesh. They are specially distributed in the southern tract of Sukma and Konta tehsils in Bastar District. In Madhya Pradesh this tribe is known as Dorla while in other two states they are popularly known as Koya. It is likely that the term 'Koya' is derived from the word "*koior koitor*". About them Thurston has told that the Koya are a tribe who inhabit the hills of north of the Godavari district and are also found in the Malkangiri taluq of the Jeypore Zamindari (Hazra, 1970). They have marital relationship with the Dorla of Madhya Pradesh.

It is told that the Dorla are one of the sub-groups of the Gond tribe of Madhya Pradesh. Hazra (1970), in his book on Dorla, mentions that the Koya are Telegu influenced Bison Horn Maria. The name Dorla, according to Grigson is a corrupt form of Dor Koitor due to their low-lying habitat. Here it is worthy to mention that the Gond prefer to introduce themselves as Koitor instead of Gond. Again the Koitor are divided into two groups, namely, the Dor-Koi or the Koitor living in the plains and the Meta Koitor or those living in the highlands. Grigson and Cain hold "the hill Koitor bears a contemptuous attitude towards the low-lying Koitor and according to Grigson the latter's tendency was to change their name from Dor-Koi or low-lying Koi to Dor-Koi or simply Dora or Dorla, a honorific Telegu word, meaning lord, 'Dora' being the singular form of Doralu" (Hazra, 1970). Therefore, from the name Dorla it is evident that the Dorla live in the plains and in low-lying habitat.

In general the Dorla habitat in the eastern and south-eastern portions is in the plains, less of forest, but when it proceeds to their north and north-western direction it becomes undulating and forested. The density of population is much more in the eastern and south-eastern parts of their habitation. Sabri river, also known as Kolab, flows through the Dorla tract. Their tract is hot and dry. In this region valuable trees such as teak, *saja, semur, tendu, aoula, palas,* toddy palm, date-palm, mahua, tamarind, mango, bamboo, catechu, siari, etc., grow abundant. The wild animals such as hyaena, jackal, spotted deer, antilope, sambar, wild boar, bear and bison, etc., are found in the forests of the Dorla tract (Hazra, 1970).

The Dorla houses are arranged in linear fashion. There is an open space in between the two rows, facing either the east or the west. The houses are encircled with kitchen garden. The houses are typically sloped and thatched with wild date-palm and toddy-palm leaves which grow profusely in their locality. The walls are made of splitted bamboo wattle and it is plastered with mud. One has to stoop to enter into the hut. Thatched roofs are slanted to protect them from rainwater and hot winds during summer. The four-sloped hut possesses an attic built at the top which serves as storing chamber of grains and cereals and this place is also used as a repository for valuable articles of the family.

Their houses are constructed with the materials available in the local forest. In their vicinity, date-palm trees grow abundantly. They use its leaves for thatching their houses.

They use mahua, sendra timber, etc., as central pillar, side poles, beams, etc. Siari leaves are used for tying, bamboo is used for making walls, doors, fencing, etc., and also the structure of the roofs. In this way, they utilise the locally available forest products in the house construction.

The Dorla are settled cultivators. The arable land is found in and around their habitat. They live in the plains, and their lands are also found in the comparatively low-lying area, suitable for paddy cultivation. "The Dorla may be said to occupy an intermediate stage of technical efficiency between that extensive nature of wet cultivation of the northern area on the one hand and shifting cultivation of the more primitive group of the Abujhmar hills and else where, on the other" (Hazra, 1970). They cultivate paddy, maize and a variety of millet. They also cultivate various types of pulses in their cultivable land. Their food chart is found to be very much balanced with their local environment. As their area is mainly the rice growing area, rice is regarded as their staple diet. They take rice in lunch and dinner, added with pulses, vegetables and if possible some non-vegetarian items too. Fishing, hunting and collection from the neighbouring forests are regarded as their subsidiary occupations. Fishing is done for their own consumption. It is preferably done during rainy season. Those who live in and are very close to jungle, sometimes go for hunting only for their own consumption except on some festive occasions when most of the men of the village go for collective hunting in the jungle. Now-a-days, they can hardly hunt any animal because thier number is decreasing day-by-day. Collection of forest products plays a vital role in their economic life. They collect various types of roots, fruits, tubers, flowers, honey, etc., which substantiate their food. Of the forest products, mahua, tendu leaves, various types of grasses such as *nulka* (by which they prepare ropes for the knitting of cots), *epur* (used to prepare broom), etc., are important. In South Bastar toddy-palm trees and tamarind grow in abundance. These grow both in their village as well as in the jungles. Tamarind has a special role in their food preparation. In that hot climate, some sour item is needed for their consumption which helps to subside the effect of heat on their body. The excess quantity of tamarind is sold in the market. Toddy-palm juice is also a very important item in their life and culture. On each and every ritual and festival, they offer the juice to the deities, along with liquor produced from mahua, which also grows in large quantity in their vicinity. Toddy-palm juice and mahua liquor are also taken by them. They have special festivals in connection with these two items.

The Dorla are endogamous. The tribe is divided into five exogamous phratries which are locally known as *gatta*. *Gatta* means group or division. The five division are Peremboi, Parem, Muro, Aido and Ero *gatta*. Each *gatta* is again divided into a number of smaller groups or clans locally called as *inteperu* or *lot peder*. These are all exogamous in nature. The persons belonging to the same *inteperu* have originated from the same god known as *pen*. They have two types of *pen* or clan god—the *baram pen* which is regarded as the supreme god of that *inteperu* and the *karra pen*—the subordinate *pen*. In a *gatta*, there are several *inteperu*. Sometimes an *inteperu* gives rise to subordinate *inteperus*. The original *inteperu* has a *pen* which is known as *boram pen* and the subordinate *pens* of the subordinate *inteperus* are known as *karra pen*. The most important function of all those phratries and clans is to regulate marriage. The clan gods have their original abode or primary seat called as *pen-rawar*. The *pen-rawar* of a clan god is situated in the village where the members of that clan have the maximum concentration. Beside the *pen-rawar* there are other secondary seats which are called as *gadde*.

The Dorla are monogamous but polygyny is not uncommon. They prefer cross-cousin marriage the most. "Marriage season usually starts soon after the harvest season is over, or towards its close, when the villagers have plenty to eat and are free from busy fieldwork" (Hazra, 1970). Here, their geographical environment has an impact in the selection of the period for the same.

In case of their religious life, the Dorla are very much particular about worship of their deceased ancestors. They have a faith in the soul after death. They hold that these are the protecting spirits. So they establish these souls in their own household and worship everyday and also on each and every ritual and festival. These souls, they believe, always guide them on right path and protect them from all the unknown dangers. Feeling of uncertainty and insecurity is there in each and every sphere of their life. The Dorla have belief in the existence of both malevolent and benevolent spirits and ghosts. They believe that sun, moon, stars, streams, rivers, hills, etc., have their own spirits. Some of them are Singanam, Garang-gubbal, Eram-raj, Bond-raj, Pajamma, Pirga-raj, Banpanamma, Boro-gubbal, Tummir-gubbal, Nerot, Masor-gubbal, Sarnam, Kaunam-raj, Ganganamma, Kuttanamma, Chil-kanni, Burug metta, Vayedoddu, Vanjal, Bal-raj, Kania, Gendraj, Chinpar, Pedapar, Chinpamul, Pedapmul, etc. The last six names are of the spirits which reside inside water (Hazra, 1970). These spirits are invoked on each and every ritual and festival. They believe that if these spirits are propitiated time to time, no harm will occur whenever they are in jungle or hills or in river.

The deities will guard them from all types of dangers and difficulties. The importance of the deities vary according to the geographical condition of the area. Those who live very close to the forest and hills, worship the deities associated with those areas and those who live very close or beside the river or any stream worship Kania, Gundraj, Chinpar, Pedapar, Chinpamul, and others.

Apart from all these deities, they have other deities such as Muttelamma, Gamam, Kora, Ganganamma and Murpu. Muttelamma is regarded as one of the very important village deities. It protects the village and the villagers from all the evils. It is invoked on all the festivals and without offering Muttelamma newly harvested crop or grain or fruit, are not taken by them it also protects them from all the unknown dangers.

The village deities vary from village to village and all of them have special functions. One of them is Chikot-raj. He is the village deity of Bhansi village. He is worshipped in the month of *Fagun* (February-March) to *Chait* (March-April) and every twelfth year his re-incarnation is observed by the villagers where previously human sacrifice was in practice. Now-a-days, it has been replaced by offering a little human blood. Other important village deities are Dubba-dev, Eram-raj, Kor-raj, etc. (Hazra, 1970).

They perform several rituals and celebrate various festivals to appease the deities. As they are mainly agriculturists, most of their rituals and festivals, locally called as *pandum*, are associated with their agricultural land and product, such as *sukkur pandum* which is a festival associated with first eating of beans. It is done during *Maga* (January-February) after the harvest of the product. After performance of *sukkur pandum* they are permitted to consume the product. It is told that during the months *Jaisth* (May-June) to *Ashar* (June-July) they perform *vija pandum*, when they worship their own agricultural land prior to seed sowing. They worship Gamam, Muttelemma and other village deities connected with the village land. They worship them to get bumper crop out of their blessings. Similarly, *amo pandum* is performed in the month of *Bhado* (September-October), when they worship Kora, Gamam and Muttelemma. It is performed just after the harvest of *amo*—a variety of millet. They worship all the deities specially the Gamam. Muttelemma, Karra and other village deities are worshiped during another festival called *korta pandum*. It is the festival associated with first rice eating ceremony, performed during the month of *Katik* (October-November). Rice is their staple food. So this festival has a special significance for these people. They never eat even a single rice grain without offering it to the deities.

There are other *pandums* such as *marka pandum* which is associated with the first eating of mango. In their area, there are plenty of toddy-palm trees. Toddy-palm juice locally known as *tar* is a very important juice. On every ritual and festival offerings of *tadi* is compulsory. It helps them to keep their body cool during the hot summer season. The festival is celebrated during the month *Fagun* (February-March) just prior to the start of summer season. It is done to accelerate the supply of toddy juice.

Similarly, they perform *sal pandum* to celebrate the offering of first collected mahua flower to their own deities. It is performed during the month of *Chait* (March-April). After the festival they are permitted to take the flower for their own consumption. The mahua trees are found in plenty in their locale. So it has importance in their day-to-day life. They take it sometimes as breakfast, sometimes as liquor. They exchange it with other essential items. It is a very important item for ritual offerings.

In this way, the Dorla life is adjusted with their local geographical niche. Their culture has grown up balancing with the local environment so that the people may survive in and may utilise the particular environment in the best possible way.

Island Tribe

Nicobarese[*]

Nicobarese are the found in Andaman and Nicobar Islands. They are of Mongoloid origin. According to 1981 census, they numbered 21,956. They are scattered in twelve islands of Nicobar, namely, Car Nicobar, Chowra, Teressa, Bimpoka, Katchall, Kamorta, Trinket, Kondul, Little Nicobar, Great Nicobar, Naneowrie, and Pulomilo (Sahay, 1981). The island is surrounded by thick forest and this forest and the sea have greatly influenced the life and culture of the island inhabitants—the Nicobarese. The Shompen Great Nicobar live is in dense forest; till date they are known as hunters and food-gatherers.

The cultural life of the tribe is strongly influenced not only by their forest niche but also the sea which plays a great role in shaping their cultural behaviour. The forests in the island is tropical. Excessive rain, proximity to the sea and sufficient sunlight facilitate thick forest and in the centre of island the forest is very thick, trees are excessively tall, which ultimately do not allow the sunlight to penetrate into the deep forest. As a result of this bushes and shrubs are grown.

The Nicobarese life is nurtured in the lap of this nature. They think that the abode of their spirit or *iwis* is in the forest. On various occasions, they try to appease the spirit by offering sacrifices. They are intimately attached with the forest since it regulates their economic life.

---

[*] This write-up is based on the published materials authored by V. Sahay (1981) and A.P. Nandan (1993).

In the following lines their dependence on forest and its impact on their lifestyle has been discussed.

The main food items they acquire from forest are coconut, arecanut, pandanus, various kinds of edible fruits, vegetables, etc. Apart from these, they also hunt wild gams from forest substantiate their food too. Since in the Nicobar Island there is abundance of coconut trees, so coconut plays a vital role in the life and culture of Nicobarese. They quench their thirst with coconut water. Coconut shells are used as toddy and water containers. They prepare toddy out of coconut flowers. In fact no part of coconut tree is left unused. The trunk of the tree is used for making stairs in their houses, the dried leaves are used for making torches which are also used for fishing and catching octopus and roasting the pigs. They also extract oil out of coconut kernel which is sold in the cooperative society to earn cash and out of this cash they purchase different articles of their domestic use. When a person dies, in his/her honour a mark of *takoya* is erected near the coconut plantation of the family. *Takoya* signifies prohibition from plucking coconut from the trees. This is marked by two sticks planted in front of coconut tree and on which a few pieces of cloth are tied and a piece of mandible of pig is hung. The number of ritual activities performed after death are expensive and to overcome this difficulty, coconuts are preserved which not only fetch them some amount of cash but are also used during various rites of death rituals. Thus, it is observed that Nicobarese not only use coconut as their food item and drink but also use it in other spheres of their life. They also make copra both for sale and domestic use.

Their huts are built within the forest with the help of forest materials like bamboo, wooden log, grasses, etc. The floor of the huts is a raised platform about 6 feet to 8 feet above the ground level and this is again supported by wooden logs. This type of hut is a kind of adaptation to the adverse ecological setting, that is, owing to plenty of rainfall and to avoid dampness of the earth. To protect them from snake and insect bite the huts are raised on platform. The staircase is removed and taken upstairs during night. It is reported that the following materials are used in their huts which they procure from neighbouring forest, viz., wooden logs, timber, coconut or arecanut trunks, bamboos and for thatching purpose grasses and coconut leaves. They also practise a series of rituals to propitate their spirits (*iwi*) by offering sacrifice of pigs and chickens during the constructing of hut. To protect them from evil eye, they keep in the corner of room a *kareyava*, which is a wooden image. The canoe is one of the important item in their life which is used for inter-island communication. Their marine economy based on catching fish, octopus for their subsistence as well as trade is fully dependent on canoe which is prepared by digging out the trunk of big tree. Baskets, mats and handmade pots are the inter-island trade items which are made of forest products. Apart from this, they also collect medicinal plants and herbs from the forest. These medicinal plants are used by their traditional medicine man for curing any disease or ailment.

Along with the forest, sea also plays an important role in shaping their socio-cultural life. They hunt various kinds of aquatic animals that are taken by them from the sea. The sea also plays a significant role in establishing their trade affair among islands.

They practise endogamy but during marital alliance they are allowed to marry anyone provided they are not related consanguineally for atleast two ascending generations. They prefer to marry within their island. However, inter-island marriages are not discouraged. Marriage between Muslim and Christian Nicobarese are common. Village as a territorial group is recognised. Their villages are always situated along the shore, and due to which the huts are surrounded by forest. Death is followed by a number of rituals. In case of unnatural death, it is believed to occur due to wrath of spirit or *iwi*. They have a death-house where they bring the old person who suffers from chronic illness for a long time. By the side of dying person, they keep *kareyavas* which is supposed to be benevolent spirit. They also place *minluana* which is supposed to protect the man from evil spirits, and the man may die in peace. They follow animistic beliefs and practices.

Due to socialisation of Nicobarese children they believe in a number of spirits—both malevolent and benevolent. On various occasions they try to appease good spirits or *lwi-ka and lwi-pat* or harmful spirits. Their belief in supernatural power and spirits or *iwi* clearly indicates nature-man interaction which ultimately shapes their culture. The impact of their physical environment is more than the impact of modernisation.

5

Food Habits and Geographical Setting

Indian tribes have adapted to natural environments. Their habitats differ as widely as hills, forests, plains, deserts, sea, islands or their combination. Their economy, social institutions, beliefs and practices and in fact their whole subsistence pattern is an adaptation to their immediate environment and their culture can be better understood in terms of their intricately interrelated nature-man-spirit complex (Vidyarthi, 1973-74).

Tribes constitute an important component of the population of India, representing about 7.6 per cent (1981 census)* of the total population of the country. They live in certain pockets with different dialects, and maintain their ethnic boundary in terms of cultural homogeneity and unique social organisation. Since these tribal groups live in secluded

---

* According to 1991 census that tribal component in India's population is 8.08 per cent.

condition, their livelihood pattern, food and dietary practices and their attitudes to various aspects of life, may often differ from those of the non-tribal population.

It is well known that topographical make-up or geographical setting of an area determines the soil condition which ultimately has tremendous influence on the local flora, cropping pattern and agricultural practices of the area. The people who live in any climatic condition have an intimate knowledge of available food resources throughout the year. Man was primarily a forest-dweller who used to depend on the forest for food and shelter. In due course when man switched over food gathering and hunting to food producing stage, he made small clearings in the forest for cultivation of cereals for consumption. Till date forest plays an important role in the life of tribals of India for food collection and gathering. Tribals living as a part of ecosystem exploit nature to meet their food demands and some of their food materials are uncommon to us. Some of their collected food materials from forest are nutritionally rich.

It is observed that a number of edible plants, tubers are used as food items which the tribal people fetch from forest. We also know that pre-historic man was largely dependent on forest for his food. Negi (1994) has classified food obtained from forest in the following categories:

(i) Food eaten only in an emergency, e.g., under famine conditions or by defense personnel whose ration supplies have been cut off or travellers who have been lost in the forest.

(ii) Wild plants gathered by people living in and around forests and eaten by them. This food is not usually available on a commercial basis.

(iii) Food gathered from the forest by the local people;

Table 4

Annual Calendar of Collection of Forest Material of Chotanagpur Tribes

Month in Local Dialect (E.E.)	Collection of Forest Materials						
	Root/Tubers	Shoot	Leaves/Vegetable	Flowers	Fruits	Seeds	Mushroom
1	2	3	4	5	6	7	8
Chait (March-April)	-	-	Munga Sag	Mahua	Ber	-	-
Vaisakh (April-May)	Gethi, Nakoa, Pitharu, Daru, Kulu, Baiyang, Baser.	-	Koenar Sag, Amit Sag, Munga Sag, Jirkan Patta, Futkal Sag, Tend Patta*	Moreja, Mahua	Amba, Jamun, Kathar, Papra, Piyar, Tend, Chihar, Mahulain, Pethu, Kachnar.	-	-
Jaith (May-June)	-do-	-	Fudina Sag, Chirkani Sag, Rote Sag, Munga Sag, Jirkan Patta, Koenar Sag, Tend Patta*.	Moreja, Mahua	Dumbar, Amba, Gular, Kathar, Kusum, Jamun, Porhu, Tut.	Sakhoa, Dori, Karanj	-
Ashad (June-July)	-do-	-	Munga Sag, Matha Sag, Katai sag, Boro Sag, Futkal Sag, Koenar Sag.	Mahua	Satalu	-do-	various type of edible mushroom

Contd...

Contd...

Month						
Sawan (July-August)	-do-	Karil	Munga Sag, Boro Sag, Kena Sag, Dail Sag, Futkal Sag, Seliar Sag.	-	Karonda, Satalu	-do-
Bhado (August-Sept.)	-do-	-do-	-do-	-	-do-	-do-
Aswin/Kuar (Sept-October)	-do-	-do-	Munga Sag	-	-do-	-
Katick (October-Nov.)	Sakhina/Sakar Kanda	-	Kohra Sag, Laua Sag, Munga Sag.	-	Kohra, Gongra	-
Aghan (Nov-Dec.)	-	-	Munga Sag.	-	-	-
Pus (December-Jan.)	-	-	Munga Sag.	-	-	-
Magh (January-Feb.)	Pitharu, Nakoa, Gethi	-do-	-do-	Jirkan, Bayer Kachnar	-	-
Fagun (Fab-March)	-	-	-do-	Mahua Ber	-	-

* Except Tend Patta (Bidi leaaves) all are food items. They also collect wood, Moreja Patta (by which they used to prepare string). Mahulain Patta and Juru Patta (For preparing rain coat and Chopi or hat), Khajur leaves (to prepare mat) and Kher grass (for thatching) throughout the year.

Note: E.E.: English Equivalent

Source: Dasgupta Samira, 1994 - Birjia: Society And Culture: Calcutta Firma KLM Pvt. Ltd.

consumed by them and also available for sale in rural and semi-urban market.

(iv) Cultivated edible forest species available for sale.

It is reported from several forest-dwelling tribes of India that they set off on their daily work of food gathering in the morning usually after taking tiffin. From forest they usually collect various edible tubers, roots, leaves and vegetables, flowers, seeds and mushrooms. These food items are seasonal. The emic view of forest and its resources are so rich among these tribal people that they can easily select a place for digging in search of tuber after observing the herbs and creepers or leaves grown on the earth. The most important of such edible tubers are *gethi* (Dioscorea bulbifera), *baser* (Indigofera linifolia), *baiyang* (Dioscorea glabra), *duru* (Dioscorea belophylla), *kulu* (Eterculia urens), *nakoa* (Momochroria vaginalis), *pitharu* (Dioscorea belophylla), *sakar kanda* (Ipomoea batatas), *sakhina kanda* (Alocasia indica, schoot), etc., taken by the Chotanagpur tribes. In case of Pando of Sarguja, Madhya Pradesh, various types of roots and tubers reported by Sinha (1981) are *bagha, birallu, bhothi, seo, gethia kanda, bajan kanda, kathua and tepna,* etc., are collected. Many of these items are also taken by the tribes of other parts of India which are known by different names.

Several leaves and vegetables are also collected by them as their food items. Some of them are *amit sag* (Bauhinia malabaica), *boro sag* (Callicarpa arborea), *chirkani sag* (Ardiscia family), *dail sag* (Portulaca quadrifida, linn), *fudina sag* (spearmint leaves or Flemingia chappar), *futkal sag* (Desmodium heterocarpum, Dc), *jirkan patta, kachnar sag* (Bauhinia tomentosa), *katai sag* (Vicoa auriculata), *kena sag* (Commelina benghalensis), *kohra sag* (Cortalaria striata De), *Koenar sag* (Bauhinia purpurea), *khajur* (Palm), *laua sag*

(Bauhinia retusa), *mahulain patta* (Bauhinia vahlii), *matha sag* (Cortalaria macrophylla), *moreja patta* (Cicer arietinum Linn), *munga sag* (Moringaceae oleifera), *rote sag* (Manihot utilissima, Pohl), *seliar sag* (Vaugunia Spinosa, Roxb). With some variations in geographical differentiation most of them are taken by the tribes all over India.

They also collect various types of seeds, flowers and fruits like *moreja* flower (Cicer arietinum), *mahua* flower (Bassia latifolia), *jirkan* flower (Citrullus vulgaris schrad), *kachnar* flower (Bauhinia purpurea Linn); fruits like *amba* (mango), *jamun* (Jam), *satalu* (pear, incase of tribes adjoining to Netarhat plateau of Bihar), *katharu* (jack fruit), *ber* (wood apple), *aonla* (Emolica officinalis), *mahulain* (Bauhinia vahlii), *kachnar, chihar* (Vitex leucoxylon, Linn), *dumbar* (Ficus hispida Linn. f), *gongra* (Luffa acgyptica), *gular* (Ficus glomerata Roxb), *karonda* (Bursera serrata), *kohra* (Garuga pinnata, Roxb), *kusum* (Schlechera oleosa), *papra* (gardenia latifolia), *piyar* (Buchanania latifolia), *pethu* (Corchorus olitorius Linn), *porhu* (Ficus cunia), *tut* (Morus alba Linn), incase of Nicobarese arecanut, coconut, *pandanus*, yams, papaya, pineapple, etc., are important. Among the common seeds collected from forest are *dori* (Bassia latifolia or Mahua), *karanj* (Pongamia pinnata), *sakhoa* (Shorea robusta or sal seed), etc. They also collect young bamboo shoot known as *bans karil;* they prepare *sabjji* out of it. There are various types of mushroom (*putu*) available in their surrounding forest, about which they possess an intimate knowledge as to, which mushroom is edible and which is not. Accordingly, they collect mushroom from forest. Among the edible mushrooms *bans khukhri and beng putu*, etc., are common. Among the tribal groups of Bastar palm juice (*tarin*) and sulphi juice (sago palm or *caryotis urens*) are easily available and are used as drinks.

Dasgupta (1994), during her study on Birjia, prepared a detailed list of materials collected throughout the year which might present a concrete picture of the tribal group.

It is also reported by Rajyalakshmi (1991) that nutrient value of some wild tubers, bamboo shoots, mushrooms consumed by the tribals (per 100 gm. edible portion) is as follows:

Table 5
Nutrient Value of Food Items Collected from Forest by the Tribals

Food Item		Mois-ture (gm)	Protein (gm)	Fat (gm)	Mine-rals (gm)	Fibre (gm)	Carbo-hydrate (gm)	Energy (kcal)
	Tuber							
A.	(i) Dioscorea bulbifera	67	3.4	1.1	0.9	0.5	27	132
	(ii) D.Pentaphylla	79	2.8	0.7	3.2	2.0	15	72
B.	Bamboo shoots processed and dried	11.6	29.6	0.4	8.5	6.9	43	294
C.	Mushroom (dried)	10.5	27.6	2.9	9.5	9.2	71	298

It is, therefore, clearly understood how forest-dwelling tribes of India are closely dependent on their forest resources for their survival. From such natural resources they not only draw the required energy for survival but also get sufficient protein, fat and minerals which are essential for existence. In different geographical settings of our country, different tribal people live and gather varied food materials from local natural resources for their survival. They have ultimately a symbiotic relation with their forest environment. The forest is also benefited from them through their various activities. Their cattles graze in the forest, cowdung becomes manure which helps to increase the fertility of soil and ultimately helps in forest growth. They burn the dried up leaves and bushes in the jungle for their convenience to pick up mahua flower. The ash becomes fertiliser and helps in forest growth. Similarly, there are several other examples where symbiotic relationship is well marked.

It is also evident that close relation between geographical environment and food habits of tribal people exists. In fact, human needs are influenced by the environment and other ecological factors prevailing in the particular niche. This is reflected in their dietary habits.

6

Religious Belief System and Environment

The tribal people under the present study mostly live in the hills, forests and in the islands, generally in isolated, less fertile and less accessible habitat. Since the tribal people live in isolation for centuries together in the desire of nature, they have developed a culture of their own adjusting with their local environment. In social and religious parts of their culture, the sun, wind, the moon, stars, trees, animals, water sources, hills, birds and the earth, etc., play a vital role. Their interaction with such natural objects became part of their great cultural heritage. In the primitive tribal groups, whatever happens in the world, any happening beyond human control or any odd in their social environment is generally attributed to the influence or mechanism of supernatural powers which ultimately resulted in the beliefs in various malevolent and benevolent spirits. To overcome all the anxieties and feelings of uncertainty believed to be created by those spirits and to get strength in mind, they perform several rituals to appease all those spirits. Ritual is nothing but the functioning or action or the performing part of religion. "Religion is one of the most important aspects of culture" (Singh, 1982) and "religion corresponds to the ecological setting to a great deal" (Chandra, 1981).

The geographical or natural environment has an overall impact on the belief system of tribal people in a particular niche. Titiev (1955) has shown the interrelationship of the universally accepted patterns of culture through the model of bio-cultural triangle where the environmental relationship of man forms the base whereas the other two arms of the triangle comprise man-man and man-supernatural (or man-social) interaction. Titiev opines that the three sides of the bio-cultural triangle are always integrated but the emphasis is not equal in all the societies (Dasgupta, 1994).

"For many anthropologists, ecology has been an explicit and prominent component of their work. Others have approached it from shadows, through the studies of cultural tradition. If one accepts the anthropological cliche that culture is the mechanism through which human beings interact with their environment, then the whole field of cultural anthropology can be characterised as human ecology. Studies of people's religious beliefs and practices implicitly, if not explicitly, address their understanding of natural process and their responses to the environmental hazards" (Milton, 1993).

It is obvious that different tribal groups possess different belief systems of their own which vary according to their local geographical environment. Their beliefs, rituals, etc., are very much associated with their life and it is difficult even to isolate or separate those from the people. In fact, these tribal people possess belief in various supernatural powers who wield a profound influence on their day-to-day life and livelihood.

The whole religious belief system among the tribal people of India may broadly be classified as (a) Sacred Geography or Territory, (b) Sacred Being, (c) Sacred Specialist, and (d) Sacred Performances.

Sacred Geography or Territory

With the utterance of the term "sacred" feelings of sanctity, purity and cleanliness automatically awaken in one's own mind.

"Vidyarthi has formulated and used terms like sacred centres, sacred segments, sacred cluster, sacred zones, sacred ground, sacred geography, to describe the social organisation of the temples. He describes the sacred complex of a place of pilgrimage, and thinks that such a concept is applicable even to tribal religion in India, with their sacred groves, sacred performance and sacred rituals" (Majumdar, 1961). Vidyarthi (1961) wrote "a sacred centre represents a single spot where a sacred performance takes place". In every tribal village there are certain places which are regarded as sacred. At those places no polluted person is allowed to keep his or her feet or touch any object lying or kept there. Those places are the abode of their creator, the heavenly father. These places are sometimes found under a big grove, specially *sal* or *mahua* or *saja* or even under some *sagun* tree. A hut is also found sometimes, constructed under such a grove or it is just an open place kept very clean and tidy. At every such place some symbols are kept. Sometimes it is a wooden log or a stone slab or an effigy or even some pebbles kept hither and thither. All these articles are anointed either with vermilion or turmeric paste added with some *aroa* (sundried) rice grains. Some *aroa* rice grains are found scattered on the floor. Small terra-cotta icons may also be found at those places. These are the places of their worship and hence regarded as sacred territory or geography. The symbols are their deities and the *aroa* rice, terracotta icons are the offerings.

There are some other places, regarded as sacred. These places are inside their own household: their cattle shed, threshing floor, and also their granary, etc. The sacred place inside the household termed as "domestic sacred centre" by Vidyarthi (1961) is generally a small chamber at a corner of the main room, partitioned from the main room by a wall. The room is specially constructed for their deceased ancestors and other family deities. It is the sacred centre where several families of the same and two or three ascending and descending generations of the same lineage together perform the rituals as per the family custom and tradition. The Birjia call the place as *ora-bhitar*. The Dorla call it *anhal* and it is *mua-asthan or sira-asthan* for the Parhaiya. Every day and on every ritual and festival they worship them with offerings to appease them. The Abuj Maria people call it as *irhu-kurwi*.

Among the Birhor, Birjia, Parhaiya, Asur and Korwa, the sacred grove is known as *sarna*. *Sarna* is "nothing but a forest growth and the place is situated just under a big sal grove" (Dasgupta, 1994).

The Abuj Maria also have the sacred place of their own, generally located under some large tree. It is known as *deogudi or talin/tallur*.

In the Nicobarese villages, there are several sacred places such as *elpenum* where all their ceremonies take place. Their birth and death houses are regarded as very important and also very sacred places for them (Sahay, 1981).

The Dorla believe that there are their sacred territories where their deities, specially the clan deities are established.

These are the *pen-rawar* and *gadde*. All the sacred territories are found situated under some large trees.

Among the Didyai there is a place under a peepal tree which is considered as a sacred territory. The place is called *bingig beer* where they perform ancestor worship (Guha, 1968).

Sacred Being

To the tribal people their deceased ancestors are believed to be their most important sacred beings. Their clan deities, their totems are also enlisted in the list of their sacred beings. They always show reverence to all of them. They never eat or kill, or even hurt their totemic items. Everyday and on every ritual and ceremonial occasion they worship their ancestors. The clan deities are also worshipped on all festivals and ceremonies.

Among their other sacred beings, *Sing-bonga* or the sun is regarded as the superiormost deity for the Birjia, Asur, Korwa, Birhor, etc. There are other deities residing in hills, forest, water sources, agricultural fields, etc. To the Birhor, moon is another very important deity called as Chandu bonga. Nanda bir presides over wind, Babsa bir presides over thunder. *Dharti mai* is worshipped by all the tribal people. The Parhaiya have a belief that *Chadi-raj* is the deity who resides in hills, *Dootho-raj* in valley, and *Chutter-raj* in plains. All these supreme beings take care of their own territory. The Korwa call the sun god as *Bhagwan*. The Birjia have a deity named *Gadidara Roeda* who lives in jungle, helps in hunting animals specially deer in jungle. Among the Abuj Maria and the Dorla their ritual cycle is guided by their own clan deities. These clan deities have their own genealogical chart and as per that the people of those clans are also related with the same kinship bondage. "The Dorla have a belief in High God or *Deur*. He resides high above in the sky. It is he who has created everything in the world" (Hazra, 1970). They also worship *purd* (sun) and *nella* (moon) in their religious ceremonies (Hazra, 1970). The Nicobarese have a belief that *iwi* (spirit) guides in all types of incidences. There are altogether eight types of *iwis*. Some of these *iwis* are responsible for all the benevolent and the rest of them are responsible for all types of malevolent acts. They have again two types of deities—the Reuse and the Minluana. The former one is considered as god who controls over all the *iwis*. Minluana is a person who has knowledge on witchcraft. In sickness or in any trouble they consult the person. (Sahay, 1981). Among the Didyai " Goesendia Hia is a god of one of the hills where they go for hunting" (Guha, 1968). Jiramolu Kitang is their another god of hills, and Bongur is propitiated as the deity of forest and is always worshipped whenever they go to the forest for hunting (Guha, 1968). Bokpa is worshipped by them to get plenty of palm juice as the deity is believed to be the god of the palm tree.

Apart from these sacred beings, there are several others who are connected with various aspects of their socio-economic life. For example, the earth deity, who is somewhere known as *Mitti deo* and somewhere as *Dharti mai* or *Tallur muttey* is worshipped by all tribal people. They worship her to get her blessings to get bumper crop. There is a deity namely, Rakshel of Korwas who protects the village from all types of evils and hazards. Korwas have another deity named Gohel residing in forest where lac grows in abundance. *Nelnarin mata* of Abuj Marias, equivalent to *Sitala mata* of Hindu pantheon is a very important deity. She protects them from all types of illness and hazards. Didyais have a belief that Raskurku—mother cult—is the deity of love. So the young unmarried boys specially worship her to get a wife like her. Among the Birhor, *Burhi mai*, a female deity is worshipped as a protector of the village and *Bagh bir*, who presides over tiger and protects them from the attack of that ferocious animals are also shown reverence. *Goreya bonga* is the presiding deity of cattle shed for the Birjia. The Dorla have several deities such as Muttalemma (who is the presiding deity of earth equivalent to *Dharti mai*), Kora and Ganganamma. All these deities are worshipped on every festivals specially connected with their agricultural cycle.

It is found in every tribal community, along with their scared beings who are benevolent for them, there are several others who are believed to be malevolent spirits. The people live in such a environment where people automatically have grown a feeling of presence of malevolent spirits. Their acts are felt through sickness, death, accident and all the types of hazards and calamities. Most of these spirits are believed as the soul of those people who died through unnatural death. Generally, like the sacred beings they are also not seen but sometimes they show their presence through some shadows, they enter into human body and try to fulfil their desire. They are very treacherous and dreadful beings. They roam here, there and every where. There are certain places where they like to stay such as burial ground or a place where a tiger killed a person, etc. The tribal people think that a pregnant woman becomes *churail* if she dies before or at the time or just after child's birth. *Darha khunt* among the Birjia is a thirsty spirit of a male child died within one month of its birth. A female child in such a case is called a *dakin*. When a person is killed by a tiger, his or her soul becomes a malevolent spirit whom the Birjia call as *Baghut* and the tribal people of Bastar call it as *Bagh duma*. The Didyai have several such spirits such as *gatsuni* (a demon), *ggsianoane ggeh* (a monkey demon), *goliasahlika* (a demon of a tree), *luli* (a fastidious demon), *nijgoli*a (a humorous demon), *papi doa golia* (wicked house demon) (Guha, 1968). In Bastar, all such spirits are called as *dand*. They are generally avoided and offered some offerings to keep them at a distance.

Among the Abuj Maria, Jhitku and Mitku also called as *gopa gosin*, are thought as very dangerous spirits. (They have a folk tale of their own where it is told that Jhitku was a poor boy. He was in love with Mitku but was unable to pay bride-price. So he was engaged as a servant in her father's house to marry Mitku by service. Once her seven brothers engaged in the construction of a dam, dreamt that if they sacrificed a boy then they easily could be able to construct it. They killed Jhitku. When Mitku came to know of it, she committed suicide at the same place and since then they became spirits). Due to their unnatural death they are listed among the malevolent spirits. The Nicobarese have many evil spirits discussed earlier.

Apart from them, there are persons who are regarded as witches. Witches guide the malevolent spirits to do harm for the persons as per their necessities and wishes. To overcome all those situations the people call and consult some specialists who are specially expert to give them relief in such critical situations. They may not be considered as sacred specialists but as they keep some connection with the supernatural world and as they prescribe the remedial measures to the people who are in distress through their magico-religious performances and also with the help of medicinal herbs, they cannot be ignored and due to this reason the authors have mentioned them in their discussion of sacred specialists.

Sacred Specialist

In every society, whether it is a tribal or non-tribal, there are some persons regarded as more skilled and knowledgeable to work as mediator between the people of the society and the deities. They work for communication between the people and the supernatural world. These are very prestigious posts. The people who hold these posts always get some special status in their society and also in the village.

In tribal societies, the sacred specialists are either selected for the post as per the order or will of the supernatural beings or on hereditary basis. These people are in general common men. They do this job as their part-time duties along with their other occupations. In all the religious functions, these people play the main role. They do prayers, offerings are made to the supernatural beings through them.

The sacred specialists are of three types, namely: (1) head of the family, (2) religious specialist of their own community, and (3) religious specialist of the village (he may be of their own community or the other living in the same village, generally hails from some dominant group). The specialists at the village and community level in some cases are categorised with some hierarchical position. In the villages where Birjias live with Oraons, generally Oraons are the dominant group. In such villages, it is very common to see the village priest hailing from the Oraon community and the Birjia priest works as his assistant.

In case of many rituals performed at family level, specially the ancestor worship, is generally performed by the male head of the family. In his absence next senior male person generally holds the post.

The Birjia call their sacred specialist as *deohar* or *dewar*. The Birhor call him as *naya* or *sokha*. The Korwa, Parhaiya and the Asur call him as *baiga*. He is a *gaita* among the Abuj Maria, and *wadde* among the Dorla. The *waddes* are of different types. Those who officiate the rituals at *pen-rawar* (permanent seat of the *pen* that is clan god), are the *pen wadde* and those who officiate the rituals at the *gadde* (temporary seat of the pen) are *gadde wadde* (Hazra, 1970). Definitely, the *pen wadde* holds the superior status than the *gadde wadde*. The Didyai call him as *pujari* or *palasi*. He is assisted by *kitang pujari* and *san pujari*, etc. The Nicobarese have different types of sacred specialists who have expertise about the supernatural world. Tamilnuana or Minluana works to drive away the evil spirits. He also cures the sick persons. Kamassun is recognised for his or her evil act, for employing evil spirits to cause harm to a person or group. Mafai, Yom Aap (guardian of a canoe), Yom Elpenum (guardian of a public house), etc., are the other spirits (Sahay, 1981).

In case of all the tribal people, beside their sacred specialists such as *pujar, deohar, pujari, wadde, gaita*, etc., (who always do the benevolent act) there are some other people who act as sorcerer and traditional medicine man called as *sirha* or *guniya* or *manti, mafai*, etc., by the studied tribal groups. These people are consulted whenever they feel that they are under the influence of some malevolent spirit. These specialists through their magical performances detect which spirit is responsible for such a trouble. They also prescribe the remedial measures. Generally, as a remedy, they ask for the sacrifice of chicken, pig, pigeon, etc. Specially, the oozed-out blood of the sacrificed animal is collected as the chief item of magical performances. These sorcerers are also responsible to call back the soul of the deceased ancestors.

Sacred Performances

Sacred performances are those which are performed to build a communication with the sacred world, through some religious performances which are always sacred. Singh (1982) named it as religious communication. In tribal societies communications are made through offerings, prayers, etc. Sahay (1981) wrote in his paper on Nicobarese that sacred performance has two aspects, one of those is ritualistic and the other is secular. The previous one consists of sacrifice, offering, driving away of evil spirits or healing a sick person. The latter one consists of eating, drinking, singing, dancing, etc. Among the offerings sacrifice of animals, offering of *daru* (liquor) are very important items. It is observed that the religious performances are directly related with the local situation. Whenever groups of people of any tribal community go for hunting, they definitely perform some rituals prior to it to appease the deities of the jungle for successful hunting expedition. As, for example, the Didyai always propitiate Bangur whenever they go to forest for hunting (Guha, 1968). Sarhul is one of the very important and gorgeous festival of the Birjia, Asur, Korwa, Parhaiya, etc., associated with forest. As they live in and around forest, forest has a very important role in their life. To adjust with the forest environment and to have a secured feeling they have got beliefs that there are deities residing in forest and if they are able to make those deities pleased with them, they will automatically be protected from all types of dangers. The Nicobarese of Andaman and Nicobar Islands live in the surroundings of sea. Fishing is one of their occupations. They often organise ceremonial and communal fishing. They perform vee-fop-lach, a festival connected with their expedition to coral reef. The Dorla live in such an ecological setup where date-palm trees grow in abundance. The date-palm juice locally known as *tarin* plays a vital role in their life. They perform *tarin pandum* once in a year to get plenty of *tarin*. Before they take the new juice they offer it to their deities to get their blessings for plenty of juice. The Dorla perform *marka pandum* prior to consuming mango during the month April. Similarly, as they start collection of *mahua*, they

perform Sal Pandum during the month of March with a hope
that they will be able to collect plenty of *mahua* flower. They
are settled agriculturists. Several rituals are performed by
them which are connected with their agricultural cycle. First,
Muttelemma mata, the Earth Goddess, is offered every
cultivated product such as beans, rice, etc., through
performance of some rituals and only after that they can
consume it. Vija Pandum is performed prior to the first
sowing of seed. In this way, the sacred performances are seen
to be very much adapted to their environmental niche.

Similarly, the Birjia have a ritual named *ora-bakhra* prior
to seed sowing. The Birjia also practise slash and burn
cultivation and there are several rituals such as *bidea, pahar
puja, jarra puja, pahar kharwaj*, etc., which are associated
with this type of cultivation. In the month of *Ashad*
(June-July) they perform *Hariar bata* to get plenty of edible
jungle products and to get bumper crop. *Rohiyat* is also
performed in *Sawan* (July-August) to get plenty of cultivated
products. During rainy season, chances of attack from insects
in the newly germinated seedlings are there. So they do *saoni
puja* to get rid of that. *Naoakhani* is performed after
harvesting of cultivated crop. They offer the new crop to
their ancestors and deities. After that they are allowed to take
it. Among the Didyai *gosandia hia* is an important ritual.
Gosandia is a god of hills where they go for hunting. They
worship him to make their arrows strong and sturdy (Guha,
1968). They do *ghia pande* which is distinguished by first
fruit ceremony. No mango is eaten before this festival (ibid.,
1968). *Osarke pande* is performed in the month of *Ashad*
(June-July) to honour the mother earth just before seed
sowing. *Rokdia hia* is performed just before ploughing to
honour the *mother earth*. She is the principal deity as she is
regarded as responsible for fertility.

In their principal rites the Didyai supplicate the mother earth and her consort, the anthill. The Didyai farmer and his wife have sexual intercourse in the fields to promote and stimulate the fertility of the fields. "The work with renewed energy in the field confident that Mother Earth has been revitalised by their copulation and will be beautiful" (Guha, 1968).

The ritual cycle of the Abuj Maria is very much connected with their own ecological background. They get plenty of mahua and it has a very important role in their ritual offerings. They never eat the newly bloomed flower without offering it to their deities. They also do the same thing with season's new mango and other fruits, vegetables and also other cereals. They perform rituals in each and every phase of their agricultural cycle such as *miching* during June-July just before sowing seed to appease the earth goddess, their ancestors and the clan deities. *Turkorta* or offering of newly harvested *tur* (a kind of millet) to the deities, *wanj korta* or offering of newly harvested paddy and *talo katla* or annual offering to earth goddess are also performed to satisfy all of their deities.

Therefore, from the above discussion, it is clear that the tribal spiritual world is completely dependent on their local environment. Their sacred grove and other sacred places (except the ancestral chamber) are established in the lap of nature, sometimes under some trees, sometimes beside a water source or on the hilltops. Their sacred beings are in general found related with hills, mountains, jungles, water sources, and also with their agricultural fields, etc. The people perform several rituals to appease them and to get blessings from them for they believe that whenever they will go for hunting in forest or fishing to river or sea or any other water source or be engaged in cultivation they will get protection from these deities and will be successful to reach the desired goal.

Through the performance of the rituals and ceremonies their dependence on nature is again marked. On every step of their agricultural operation, they perform various rituals. The offerings are mainly the newly harvested or produced crop or fruit. As there is plenty of *mahua* flower, *daru* prepared from it is an essential item of offerings to the deities. Wherever, sago palm (Caryotis urens) is grown in plenty, among their offerings liquor prepared from it is also considered as one of the offerings to the deities. In this way their dependence on their local environment is easily marked.

7

Folk Treatment of Diseases

From time immemorial, the people of India, irrespective of their cultural and technological achievement, have depended upon their immediate geographical environment, not only for livelihood, but also for various aspects in their daily life. The interaction of such people with their immediate niche, over time, enables them to understand some of the important aspects of the ecosystem which can be perceived by them only. The cultural construct of the environment, the traditional perception as well as analysis of the environment and its importance in the socio-cultural life of people may be described as ethno-ecology. The knowledge to utilise the local environmental resources by the people or by a community is mainly dependent upon their indigenous interaction with the environment which is transmitted orally from generation to generation and therefore, it is highly confined to persons. This is also known as folk medicine which is highly rich in our country and is still prevalent in many tribal groups of our country. In most cases, these tribal people are away from modern medical facility.

It is widely accepted that most ethnic groups are exploiting their environment through hunting, collection, gathering for consumption, sale or exchange of forest produce within the same geographical niche or outside (Haimendorf, 1943; Bhowmick, 1989). Apart from these they also exploit such resources during their ailment.

In the following lines the remedies of diseases are discussed. The tribal people mainly depend on their forest environment from where they collect the medicinal herbs, plants, roots, tubers, fruits, flowers, etc., to treat the ailments.

Folk Treatment of Diseases

	Disease	Way of Treatment	Tribes Involved
1.	Khuktana (cough and cold)	The root of *Tin patti* trees (Desmodium polycarpurn) is taken with water or fruit of *Banbhanta* tree (Clesodendrum indicurn) is tied on the neck of the patient as *totakah* (an empiric medicine).	Birjia (Chotanagpur)
2.	Jwar/Jendraina (fever)	(a) The bark of *Karam* (Adina cordifolia) tree is crushed and soaked in water. It is then boiled in water, added with some salt and then taken.	do
		(b) Bitter bark of *Gethi* tuber (Dioscorea bulbifera) is crushed and eaten with water.	do
		(c) When fever continues for several days then *Ghoti* tuber (Vernonia roxburghii) is rubbed on the stone and taken with water.	do
3.	Samangha Sutana (headache)	(a) Turmeric and garlic are ground together and spread on the forehead.	do
		(b) Root of *Putri* (Coton roxburghii) tree is rubbed and applied on the forehead.	do
4.	Hatta/Ulti (vomiting)	The root of *Umarjoni* tree is ground along with red onion and taken with water.	do

Contd...

Contd...

5.	Suantana (stomachache)	(a) The root of *Aithu* (Grenia tiliae folia) tree is crushed and taken with water.	do
		(b) Bark of *Arjun* (T.arjuna) tree is ground and boiled in water and consumed. The paste is applied on the abdomen.	do
		(c) The root of *Tin patti* (Desmodium polycarpurn) tree or root of *Marodotto* (Helictores isora) tree or bark of *Tilsa* (Sterculia urens) tree is crushed to powder and then taken with water.	do
6.	Data hasua (toothache)	Root of *Rangaina* creeper (Solanum xanthocarpum) is crushed and made into paste and applied to the affected tooth.	Birjia (Chotanagpur)
7.	Haddi tutna (fracture of bone)	(a) The *Harjorni* (Cissus quadrangula linn) leaves are tied on the affected region and its paste is also applied on the region. Then the bone is tied with the help of bamboo, woods and string for a fortnight.	do
		(b) *Dudhi Kanda* (Hemidesmus indicus) is crushed into paste and mixed with *mahua* (Bassia latifolia) liquor and the substance is taken. The broken portion of the bone is tied with the help of bamboo, wood and string for a fortnight.	do
8.	Gethia (rheumatism)	Powdered *Champa* (Michelia champaca) root is taken with water.	do
9.	Aonkatitana (dysentry)	(a) Sarai (Sal) seeds are crushed and taken with water.	do
		(b) Bark of mango tree or *Tilsa* (Sterculia urens) tree is crushed and taken with water.	do
10.	Suobai (blood dysentery)	Sarai (Sal) seeds are crushed and taken without water.	do
11.	Ghava (wounds/cuts)	(a) Apply *Kusum* (Schlechera oleosa) oil on the affected part.	do
		(b) Apply powdered bark of *Chairpain* (Desmodium Sp.) tree mixed with water.	do
		(c) Apply *Chhathir* (Alstonia scleolaris) root on the affected part after grinding.	do
12.	Foka (burns)	(a) Apply the fat of bora snake on the burns.	do

Contd...

Contd...

		(b) Ashes of burnt cloth is mixed with *Karanj* (Pongamia pinnata) oil and applied on the burns. Then after a while, washed in water.	do
13.	Sujak (blood in urine)	Setha (Annona squamosa) root or *Karhi* (Capparis decidua) root is crushed into paste and taken with water.	do
14.	Banjhi (barrenness)	The root of the *Balkumhi* (Strychnos potatorum) tree is rubbed with stone and taken with cold water.	do
15.	Garra Girana-ko (abortion)	After crushing the young shoots of *Dhandhapoi* (Rivea hypocrateriformis) it is taken with one quarter bottle of mahua liquor.	Birjia (Chotanagpur)
16.	Snake bite	(a) Prepare ointment of *Chirchina* (Panicum miliaecum linn.) grass and apply on the bitten place.	Birjia (Chotanagpur)
		(b) Apply, ground *Katpan* (Ehretia lacvis) root and tie the place above the bitten place tightly.	do
		(c) Massage a paste prepared from the fat of snake mixed with fat of *Goir* animal.	do
17.	Cold and disorder of digestive system	Juice of *Makaibi* (Drymaria cordata) plant is used as laxative and also taken in case of disorder of digestive system. Leaves roasted and inhaled by them which recover them from cold.	Toto (West Bengal)
18.	Diarrhoea	Juice of *Sadhimodi* root (Emilia sonchifolia) is used.	do
19.	Fever	Juice of *Pagra* (Laportea erenulate) root is taken.	do
20.	Small Pox and fracture	Powdered leaves of *Harsoo* (Pothos scandens) are applied in case of small pox. While stem made into paste and used as poultice on the fractured part of the body.	do
21.	Check bleeding from wounds	Grind the plant of *Duba* (Cynodon dactylon) and apply its juice on the affected region.	do
22.	Scorpion bite	The bark of *Langaya* (Polyalthia simiaram) or *ahmiche* (Amaranthus viridis) is ground and applied as paste or juice of leaves are applied.	do

Contd...

Contd...

23.	Stomach trouble	Bark juice of *Lungdi* (Glochidion assamicum) is taken.	do
24.	Fever	(a) Extract of the stem of *Guruch* (Tinospora cordifolia) is consumed.	Halba, Bhatra of Bastar
		(b) Whole plant extract *Kalabhuili* (Andrographic paniculata) is taken.	do
25.	Snake bite	Root extract of *Hiran Khuri* (Cissampelos parerira) are dropped in ear as well as root extract paste are rubbed in the affected parts.	Dandami Maria and Bhatra of Bastar
26.	Irregularity in Mensuration	Root extract of *Jangli Kapas* (Gosaypium hirsutum) is consumed.	Bhatra, Halba of Bastar.
27.	Urinary trouble	Root extract of *Zintijhari* (Abutilon indicum) is consumed.	Dhurwa, Halba and Bhatra of Bastar
28.	Wound due to burn	Paste of *Charpak* (Buchinamia lansan) bark is applied.	Dandami Maria, Bhatra of Bastar
29.	Headache and blood pressure	Leaves of *munga* (Moringe oleifera) are boiled and taken with water.	All the tribes of Bastar
30.	Bone fracture	(a) Bark of *Kahu* (Terminalia arjuna) Plant is boiled and added with milk and taken.	Bhatra, Halba, Dhurwa, Muria of Bastar.
		(b) After grinding the stem of *Hadgod* (Vitis quadrongularis) pulp is applied on the affected parts.	do
		(c) Bark of *Maidchal* (Litsea sebifera) is used as paste on the affected parts.	Halba, Maria of Bastar.
31.	Skin diseases	Neem (Asadirachla indica) oil is extracted from the fruit and applied on the affected parts.	Halba, Bhatra Dhurwa of Bastar.
32.	Abortion	(a) The root of *Chitrak* plant (Plumbago zeylanica) is used. The scales and bark of the root are removed and cleared. This plup is then wrapped in a cotton which is mounted on a small stick (stick of match-box) and then the pulp is dried and inserted into the vagina.	Halba, Bhatra Dhurwa of Bastar.

Contd...

Contd...

		(b) Root extract of *Kalihari* (Gloriosa superba) is consumed.	Dandami Maria and Muria of Bastar
33.	Cough	(a) Juice of *Bagarlyata* (Adhatoda vasica) leaf and flowers are consumed.	Bhatra, Muria Dhurwa of Bastar.
		(b) Leaf and fruit of *Bohar* (Cordia myxa) are used.	Bhatra of Bastar
		(c) Fruit of *Vejribhata* (Solanum indicum) is used.	Halba of Bastar
34.	Dental infection	Juice of root of *Bajradanti* (Barleris cristata) is applied on the affected parts.	Bhatra, Dandami Maria of Bastar.
35.	Cough and cold	Plant extract of white *Tulsi* (Ocimum sanctum) is consumed.	Dhurwa, Muria Bhatra, Halba of Bastar.
36.	Diarrhoea	(a) Whole plant juice of *Chota dudhi* (Euphorbia hirta) is consumed.	Dhurwa, Dandami Maria of Bastar.
		(b) Seven grains of rice and seven grains of *Urad* pulse and a dry leaf of any old bamboo are ground together, boil in water then strain and consumed in empty stomach.	Muria of Bastar.
37.	Secretion of Sufficient milk of new born's mother	Root extract of *Satawar* plant (Asparagus recemosus) is consumed or the root is directly consumed.	Bhatra, Dandami Maria, Dhurwa of Bastar.
38.	Burn	Paste of the bark of *Dumar* (F. glomerata) plant is applied	Dandami Maria Abuj Maria, Halba of Bastar.
39.	For cracked feet and wound in the ear of bullock	Extract oil from the fat of *Dhaman* snake and cobra snake and apply on the affected parts.	Muria of Bastar.
40.	Headache	Grind up the roots of *Makar* and *Tikur* (Curcuma augustifolia) with fresh *Haldi*, make a hot poultice of this and apply it on the head.	Muria, Halba Dhurwa of Bastar.

Contd...

Contd...

41.	Yaws	Collect some *Harra* fruit (myrobalams), dry and grind them into powder. Make a paste with a little oil and apply on the sores.	Abuj Maria of Bastar.
42.	Rheumatism	(a) Oil extracted from fatty parts of tiger, leopard or bear is believed to be effective which is applied on the affected parts.	Muria of Bastar
		(b) Touch the painful swelling with a bit of 'Seed-iron' (bij Loha) or a thunderbolt.	Muria of Bastar
43.	Mad dog bite	Get a piece of flesh of a mad dog which has expired, dry it carefully and store it. In case of necessity, the small piece of such flesh (not less than 2 years old) is mixed with molasses and consumed.	Muria of Bastar
44.	Safe delivery	Root extract of *Larjera* (Achyranthes aspera) is consumed.	Dorla, Dhurwa, Dandami Maria of Bastar
45.	Snake bite	The gall blader of *Bagum* fish is used. The Muria extract the gall bladder and preserve it by filling it with the small Kosra grain. They keep it carefully and when it is needed the grain soaked in the bladder secretions is removed and put in water and when it is dissolved, it is given to the patient to drink.	Muria of Bastar
46.	Abortion	The Juice of a newly tapped tree of Sago palm usually avoided by the pregnant woman.	Muria, Bhatra, Abuj Maria Halba of Bastar.

It is clear from the above discussion, that indigenous systems of medicine to treat various ailments among Indian tribes depend upon their forest environment. It is also evident that they have intimately observed their geographical environment for their survival. Different Indian tribes have distinctive ethno-medicinal practise which persist even though modern medicare is available to them. Therefore, it would be wise to cultivate this arena of knowledge widely in order to develop a new horizon in the medical field. Thus, the above information is highly valuable as it has developed among the tribals over generations. So, it is time for academicians, scientists, planners, NGOs, to take care to practise and to initiate proper documentation of tribal medicine in a more scientific way.

8

Folk Tradition in Forest Management

Most of the tribal communities in our country have been living in forest areas for a long time. Having lived in isolation in the natural setting, they have developed cultures of their own. Nature, especially trees, animals, birds, etc., has become part of their totem and their experience with nature are part of their glorious mythology. Their dependence on nature was total in ancient times when they were supposed to be "lord of forests".

With the introduction of first Forest Act by the British, the tribal's rights of forest were withdrawn. After independence, the government has given them some privileges by allowing collection of fuelwood, grazing of cattle and collection of minor forest produce for sale, etc., but the tribals continued to feel deprived from their natural right. With the implementation of Forest Act 1980, forests became practically "out of bounds" for tribals.

Tribals of our country still love to live in their original,

natural abode consisting of hills, forests, rivers, fresh air, soil
and practise their traditional way of living, rituals, customs,
dance, music, and traditional belief system of health cure
within their self-sustained forest ecosystem. Their traditional
beliefs and practices have helped them in the preservation of
their age-old culture and along with it in the conservation of
the physical environment, biological and ecological legacies
which have come to present day as a great heritage from these
primitive people. With the onset of industrialisation,
urbanisation the age-old culture of these primitive people is
being threatened since their way of life is fostered in the lap
of nature and forest which is changing rapidly due to
deforestation.

The tribals are in close interaction with forest
environment, perhaps due to this Birjia of Chotanagpur are
often known as "fish of the jungle". In fact, they are an
integral part of the forest ecosystem and like the other
components of terrestrial ecosystem they have been playing a
significant role in the operation of forest ecosystem and in the
maintenance of the ecological balance in the area.

They have a symbiotic relationship with the forest since
time immemorial. From the forest, they derive their basic
needs of survival, i.e., food materials like fruits, nuts,
vegetable leaves, various types of tubers and roots,
mushrooms, etc., for themselves. Forest is also a source for
their shelter, collection of raw materials for their huts,
firewood, fibres for clothing (in case of Bondo tribe of
Orissa), rope, wood, bamboo and grass for housing and
farming, grazing of their cattle, herbal medicine for health,
and earning source through the sale or barter of gums, resins,
waxes, honey, *chiranji* seed, *mahua*, silkworm cocoons
(*kosa*),tamarind, *phooljharu* (for Abuj Maria), sal seed, sindur
seed, mushroom, *bora, bans karil*, chirata—a kind of

medicinal plant and several other valuable forest products. In turn they protect the forest with their folk knowledge and also enrich its fertility through their various cultural performances, beliefs and practices. The forests not only give livelihood to the tribals but also provide them with social bondage and a culture reminiscent of their ancestors. Rajiv Sinha (1991), in his article "Ecosystem Preservation Through Faith and Tradition in India", observes that tribal women think of forest as their *maika* and the trees are held sacred; He writes that although the tribal people cut some trees in the forest for economic and other purposes, side-by-side they take the vow of planting new trees in the vicinity of their habitat to keep up the ecological balance.

It has been observed that tribal people of Bastar often collect fuelwood or timber for their houses but they never cut the whole tree. They allow it to grow and germinate in the next couple of years.

Cognisance of Environment

A close observation speaks that the long stretched deciduous forest from Bastar, Koraput, Khambam to Chotanagpur area of Bihar more or less possess a similar ecological condition. The perceptions of environment by the forest dwelling tribes in these forests are almost similar. Abuj-Maria of Bastar cognise their environment along with their ritual cycle. For example, as soon as Kaksar festival is performed among Abuj Maria, they think about onset of monsoon; and when *mahua*, *palash* flowers bloom, they think summer is approaching. In fact, this sort of knowledge can only be acquired due to intimate association with immediate environment which is otherwise known as cognisance of environment.

Folk Tradition in Preserving Biodiversity

Animism, naturalism, various beliefs and practices are part of the cultural life of the tribals in India. In their system plant, animals, hills, trees, rivers, lakes, ponds, stones, mountain tops, etc., are considered sacred. Nature worship is a form of belief and all nature's creations have to be protected. In fact, this sort of dependence on nature has greatly helped in the preservation and protection of many natural items of ecosystem in our country. Due to such belief several "virgin forests" or a patch of land have survived in its pristine glory. These are sacred groves, usually dedicated to a deity or the Mother Goddess who is supposed to protect and preside over the groves and intruders will be punished. These sacred groves in Chotanagpur are known as *sarna* or *jaher asthan* among Santal, Birjia, Munda, etc., and *tallur, talin, deogudi* among tribal people of Bastar or *gossaiyan* (a kind of spirit lives under a tree) or *manjhi than* among Maler of Santal Pargana.

These virgin forests also preserve several wild species of biologically diverse flora and fauna. Since many of them are on the verge of extinction, their survival in these sacred groves is of great ecological significance for the biosphere. For example one significant medicinal plant *Rawolfia serpentina* yielding 'reserpine' drug for the treatment of high blood pressure and which has disappeared from nature are found only in sacred forests preserved by the tribals (Sinha, 1995). In fact, these patches of forests in the abode of forest-dwelling tribes contribute significantly in the maintenance of biological diversity and ecological balance of the country. The sacred groves of ancient times have became the 'biosphere reserve' of today and are found in several parts of country.

It has been observed that tribals are highly conscious

about their local environment and resourceful plant, trees. They never destroy *mahua, kusum* tree, *sulphi, aden* and even *sal* trees are protected in view of economic and ritual value in their subsistence pattern. In order to check soil erosion the tribals of Bastar avoid uprooting of any tree from forest. Yes, they often cut the tree for timber use but never uproot it.

Forest-Environment Management

The fate of economy of the forest-dwelling tribes is in many ways interlaced with the forest. Forest-based tribal development should be encouraged. Shifting cultivation is one of the chief areas of subsistence among forest-dwelling tribes. The shifting cultivation has various evil effects which are as follows:

1. It destroys the valuable forests.

2. It leads acute soil erosion.

3. It causes spring below the hill to dry up.

4. It causes heavy floods down the river endangering life and property.

If the forest-dwelling tribes are involved in some economically gainful arena, then it is possible for better management of forest because in such cases tribals are themselves attached with such programmes. For instance, the tribal people can come out with their expertise in extraction of various forest products by which both the tribals as well as the forest department may be benefited. Various kinds of employment opportunities may be generated by the forest authorities for the tribals. Wildlife sanctuary has also helped in preserving biodiversity in the tribal tracts.

The development of these tribals should be thought in the perspective of local niche which means exploitation of local natural resources by which one can economically be benefited and at the same time balance of ecosystem may be maintained. For instance, in the tribal abode of Bastar, one can think to develop social forestry by planting trees like *sajas* or *aden*, tamarind, *mahua*, baniyan, *jagdumar*, *sulphi*, *chiran*ji, *aonla*, sagun, sal, arjun, etc. In case of *saja*, baniyan, *jagdumar* tree, it has some religious importance while fruit bearing trees as well as *mahua* tree have economic importance among them. They usually avoid to cut those trees in their niche.

9

Ecology and Development

"The concept of an ecosystem emphasises the material interdependencies among a group of organisms which form a community and the relevant physical features of the setting in which they are found; and the scientific task becomes one of the investigating the internal dynamics of system and the ways in which they develop and change" (Geertz, 1963). The basic unit of ecology rests on ecosystem which is again related with animals and plants of its physical environment. Man has direct and indirect interaction with his physical environment and this consequently gives a typical way of life in a specific geographical environment.

Both culture and ecology are the conceptual terms which have occupied central position in cultural anthropology during the last half of the 19th century and the middle of 20th century. Gradually, the term 'ecology' came into limelight to understand cultural development and the process of transformation.

Recently, in early part of the year 1997, there was

tremendous media attention towards 'Malik Makbuja Tree Scandal' at Bastar. It is well-known that in Bastar there are thick forests accommodating valuable timbers. As per the district authority of Bastar, 55 per cent of its area is under forest, which has the pride of having 15 per cent of forests in Madhya Pradesh. But for the last couple of years it has been reduced to 30 per cent only. This forest has an unique biodiversity which is famous in the country. Corruption in the administrative machinery results into radical illegal felling of trees and ultimately a serious threat environment. In fact, the tribes of Bastar are directly related with their ecosystem—their subsistence pattern, and the socio-cultural behaviour are governed by the ecology.

The historical background of forest speaks that the aborigines have been closely related with the forest since they are nourished in the lap of nature. Their life is intimately linked with the forest which is their well-loved habitation and source of livelihood. These tribals have enjoyed freedom to use forest and to hunt animals. They think that it is their natural right to get sustenance from the forests. Forests give them food and shelter. Edible fruits of all kinds, leaves, roots, tubers, mushroom, animals, birds, insects and fish from rivulet and streams of the forest constitute their food items. Forests also provide raw material for erecting their huts. Their cattle graze in the forests. In case of ailment they depend on herbal plants which they procure from the forests. Forest keeps them warm with fuel, cool with shade and are a source of ingredients for their alcoholic drink. In addition, hunting of wild game and fishing are common among them. This sort of association with the forests from early days to till date gives birth to a deep feeling in their mind that forest is their own. They have used the forest lands for cultivation as per their desire. But the age-old system of their right over forest has started to change when gradually people from outside moved into the forests in the middle of 19th century (Report of the Scheduled Areas and Scheduled Tribes, Dhebar Commission, Vol.I, 1960-61). Many of the tribal customary laws in respect of cultivation, hunting were found to be inconsistent with conservation and were considered detrimental to the society. Therefore, the government policy is to control and regulate the privileges and rights enjoyed by the users. In this process, tribals have been deprived of some of their natural rights over forests.

A functional classification of forests has been made by Roy Burman (1968), basing on major National Forest Policy of India, 1952, which is as follow:

(a) Protected forests, i.e., those forests which must be preserved or created for physical or climatic considerations.

(b) National forests, i.e., those which have to be maintained and managed to meet the needs of defense, communication, industry and other purposes for public interest.

(c) Village forests, i.e., those which have to be maintained to provide firewood, to release cowdung for manure and to yield small timber for agricultural implements and other forest produce for local requirements and to provide for grazing of cattle.

(d) Free lands, i.e., those areas which, though outside the scope of the ordinary forest management, are essential for the amelioration of the physical condition of the country.

While making the above functional classification of forests, six dominant needs of the country were also identified by government which are as follow:

(a) the need for evolving a system of balanced and complementary landuse;

(b) the need for checking

   (i) denudation in mountainous areas,

   (ii) erosion on the treeless banks of great rivers,

   (iii) invasion of sea sands, on coastal tracts and shifting sand dunes in the desert;

(c) the need for establishing tree lands for ameliorating physical and climatic condition;

(d) the need for ensuring supplies of grazing material, small wood for agricultural implements, etc;

(e) the need for sustained supply of timber and other forest produces required for defense, communication and industry; and

(f) the need for realisation of the maximum annual revenue.

It is also enunciated that the reserved forests are permanently retained as government forests and the neighbouring community is hardly given any right over them while the protected forests are burdened with rights of the neighbouring people but cannot be deforested without prior approval of the forest department and the forest authorities have the right to prohibit entry into the forest for a period not exceeding 30 years.

The state government may also assign to any ethnic group of village the rights of the government to or over any land which has been declared a reserved forest and may cancel such assignment. All forests so assigned are known as village forests (Roy Burman, 1968).

Apart from these, there are some other forests in some states of India like: (i) unclassed—which is controlled by forest department and profusely used by the neighbouring ethnic groups as they have right to cut trees and allowed to graze their cattle, (ii) private forest—it is usually less than 50 acres in size and scattered.

In fact, the inhabitants, in most of the forest regions, are tribals and the forest policy and law affect their socio-cultural life. Bearing the above facts in mind, some privileges and rights are given to tribals for exploiting such resources in view of their subsistence pattern and socio-religious practices:

(a) Concessions and Privileges in Respect of Cultivation

In Andaman and Nicobar Islands, the tribals are permitted to practise cultivation in different forest patches. In Gujarat, forest lands are granted to forest-settlers. These lands are also inherited by the sons from their father. In Madhya Pradesh, the Bhaina who live in wild forest tract between Satpura range and the area south of Chotanagpur Plateau, practise agriculture in the forest. The Abuj-Maria or Hill-Maria of Bastar District of Madhya Pradesh are allowed to cut the trees and clear the patch of land for *beonra* (slash and burn cultivation).

(b) Concessions and Privileges Regarding Grazing

In Madhya Pradesh, the people living in forest areas have traditional right to graze their cattle in the forest. The tribals living in the protected forests throughout Madhya Pradesh have retained some privileges regarding grazing their cattle. In Orissa, it has been reported that grazing of cattle in reserved forest was permitted on payment of prescribed fees (Roy Burman, 1968).

Apart from these, for the forest-dwelling people the concession and privileges are also extended to collect fuelwood, timber, bamboo and grasses for construction of huts, hunting of small games like hare, birds, etc., fishing, collection of minor forest produce, like, bamboo for basketry, bark of trees for making ropes, *phoolbuhari* (broom) which grow profusely in Abuj-Marh area. *Kosa* (silk cocoons), tamarind, *mahua*, medicinal plants, fruits, sal seeds and *chiranji*, etc., are collected and also allowed to be sold or exchanged in the weekly market, for earning their livelihood.

Since centuries, the terms 'tribe' and 'forest' are so closely interrelated that a symbiotic relationship exists between them. Our study clearly states that forest environment plays a chief role in shaping the socio-economic and religious life of the tribal people, hence forest to the tribals may be conceived as heart of their livelihood. The Indian Forest Act, 1865 and 1878 affirmed the state right over the forests and monopoly over their utilization. The National Forest Policy, 1952 could not serve their expectation though some concessions and privileges were granted. The tribals feel displeased and indignant due to the complete denial of ownership status of forest land to them which has been under their virtual control over generations. The National Forest Policy, 1988 states that shifting cultivation has direct adverse impact on forest environment and productivity of land. Considering suitable landuse pattern for their sustenance the National Forest Policy, 1988 has discouraged the shifting cultivation. But nothing has been done. It is true at least from our observation from Bastar district of Madhya Pradesh and many areas of Chotanagpur plateau of Bihar and Malkangiri district of Orissa that forest is damaged or destroyed by the officials mercilessly in the name of revenue collection, developmental work or project rehabilitation, etc. In this regard the tribal feeling is "by virtue of acquiring official power and in the name of development and revenue, they are destroying forest wealth ruthlessly. We feel that we are nourished in this lap of nature, and we have right over generation. But it is not acknowledged by the authority." These feelings of negligence and injustice arouse a strong sense of tribalism among them which may turn violent in future against the authority. The genesis of Jharkhand movement may be cited as an example in this regard.

"The tribal people are an integral part of the forest ecosystem and like the other components of terrestrial ecosystem they have been playing a significant role in the operation of the forest eco-system and in the maintenance of the ecological balance in an area. The forest resources not only give livelihood to the tribals but they also provide them with a social bond and a culture reminiscent of their ancestors. The tribal culture is inexorably woven around the forest. The tribal women regard forest as their *maika* (father's home) and the trees are held sacred" (Sinha, 1995). "Even if a tribal cuts a tree or clears some patch of forest for making a home and farm, they (i.e., tribal) take the vow of planting several times more trees than those removed" (Sinha, 1991).

Traditional Way of Preserving Biodiversity

The religious pantheon plays a great role in the tribal life for preserving their geographical environment. In fact, in their culture, plants, animals, trees, rivers, stones and hills are considered sacred and these are protected. The faith of these tribes has greatly helped in the preservation and the protection of many natural objects in the ecosystem of the country. For instance, as per their customary law it is tabooed to kill or hunt or eat the totemic object by which fauna and flora are preserved in the forest. They have sacred groves like *sarna* or *jaher asthan* of Santal, Kharia, and Munda of Chotanagpur area which is a seat of village god and it consists of a patch of forest where old trees are standing and this patch of forests is left untouched by the inhabitants. Any sort of interference into it is totally tabooed in the name of their religious belief system. This place is usually dedicated to a deity or mother goddess who is supposed to protect them against any calamity and ensure the fertility of soil and welfare of the people and the cattle. Hence, it is sacred and anyone who disregard the grove are punished as per their belief system. The Gond of Central India prohibit the cutting of tree, but only fallen branch can be used (Jain, 1986). In some forests of our country, even the dry foliage and the fallen fruits of trees are not touched (Sinha, 1995). In fact, the idea of the sacred groves of pre-historic days have become the 'biosphere reserves' of today and are found in various corners of our country in order to preserve and protect the ecosystem.

II

Cognisance of Environment

Close observation reflects that the long stretched deciduous forest from Bastar (of Madhya Pradesh), Koraput (of Orissa), Khambam (of Andhra Pradesh) area to Chotanagpur belt of Bihar more or less possess a similar ecological condition where the perception of environment by the forest-dwelling tribes in these hard-wood forest are almost similar. The tribes of Bastar cognised their environment along with their ritual cycle. For instance, as soon as *kaksar* festival is performed among Abuj-Maria they think about the onset of monsoon which will continue till October when Dushera will be observed and after Dushera winter start and when *marai* or *madai* festivals in the month of January or February and Holi in March are performed and when *mahua* flower blooms they think it is the period of summer. It is also reported by Adhikari (1984) that the Birhor divide the universe into two parts, viz., *rimil* or sky and *utaye* or earth. To the Birhor, the earth is round-shaped and flat surfaced while the sky is a hollow concave structure overarching it. According to Birhor worldview the, *utaye* is further divided into *muluk* (non-forested area) and *disum* (forested area). The Birhor also divided the seasonal variation into *rabang* (winter), *shitang* (summer) and *jargi* (rainy). During *rabang*, they do not face any food crisis because during these days forest is full of resources, monkey as a prey is easily available, they feel cold when the days become shorter, when they observe that mango tree and sal tree, etc., are likely to start blooming, they feel *shitang* is approaching. During *jargi* season, hunting and collection become difficult.

Birjia—a less known primitive forest-dwelling tribe of Chotanagpur plateau of Bihar—cognise their environment in the following way: the Birjia divide the year into *garmi* (summer), *barkha* (monsoon) and *jara* (winter) seasons . Celebration of Holi festival and blooming of sal and *mahua* flowers marks the outset of summer. A few days later, the sal flowers begin to fall which are collected and stored by the people to get seed out of the flower; falling of sal flower stop in the rainy season with the appearance of wet clouds in the sky. With the performance of *sohorai* (a ritual for cattle in the month of October-November) they believe that winter is setting in. It is also observed by Dasgupta (1994) that absolute dependence on the ecological setting for pursuing their economic, cultural and ritual activities is related to their natural environment. Their existence and the process of enculturation are highly influenced by forest environment (Dasgupta, 1994).

In this context, Roy Chaudhuri's (1980) observation on fisherman's perception of their immediate environment regarding catching of fish is remarkable. Since catching of fish is their only source of livelihood, they have exploited their whole knowledge regarding behavioural pattern of fish and their habitation in water. The water colour of the sea varies according to depth and chemical contents. Where the water colour looks like juice of mango steen (reddish in colour) in the month of November-December or December-January between 6th and 9th lunar days when the current is low, they call it *gab-jal*, when *med, bhetki, bhola, lakshya (silang)* fish are found. The blue water is an important sign for fishing folk. At some places of blue water, sparkling lights are seen in the night due to phosphorus content in the water, this type of water is known as *juni-bhang jal* where fishes like *hilsa, phesa, domla and rupapati* are found in good quantity.

In fact, this sort of knowledge can only be acquired due to intimate association with the immediate environment which is otherwise known as cognisance of environment. These tribal and rural people without any formal knowledge acquire this sort of knowledge over generations through oral tradition. They do not have any institution to learn these knowledge and propagate the same to the younger generations. It is our duty to document all such traditional knowledge and try to establish scientific background of such knowledge.

III

To our mind, the term 'development' in the perspective of ecology means exploitation of local natural resources by which one can economically be benefited and at the same time balance of eco system may be maintained. In fact, in the name of national interest the idea of the development programme is usually conceived by the elite class and the politically dominant group. Most of the developmental programmes of government, despite spending huge amount and displacing a large number of people from their traditional moorings, have failed to achieve the desired targets. In fact, due to such programmes the tribals have lost their land and on the contrary the nation has gained nothing; rather a lot of problems have been created. In any developmental programme, the natural resources cannot be ignored. These natural resources must be properly harnessed to facilitate the process of development.

For better management of natural environment and to keep eco-balance, one should always take care of the preservation of the natural resources along with its sustainable use.

The forest resources are considered as revenue earners for the state. In the economic sphere forest has two parts: forestry and logging. Forestry includes social forestry and conservation, gathering of uncultivated material, charcoal preparation, while logging includes felling and cutting of trees, hewing or shaping of poles and transportation of logs. The revenue can also be earned through minor forest products like bamboo, kendu leaves, lac, *kosa* (cocoon), tamarind, wild turmeric, mahua, *madh* (honey), chiranji, sal seed, resin and *phool jharu*, etc. Among the major forest products through which revenue is earned are: (i) industrial wood (a) where timber is shaped into various sizes for commercial use, (b) pulp wood, etc., and (ii) fuelwood which includes firewood and charcoal wood, etc. In all the sectors of forestry and timber work, the forest-dwellers are engaged, that is, people's participation is observed by which they may earn to substantiate their livelihood. On the other hand, the forest department also earns a substantial amount as state revenue.

Bearing the above sector of earnings in mind, the importance should be laid on forest-based industries where forest-dwellers' or tribal participation will also be encouraged. In this way, their per capita earning will increase and their feeling towards social or geographical isolation from the main stream of Indian population will also be eradicated. For developmental part, the 'emic' approach or 'insiders approach', will be more suitable because they will always know more than we do about their needs. Apart from this, when they participate in such developmental programmes, they will consider it their own which is a positive point for any developmental programme. We feel, only in this way, welfare and developmental activities can be best launched.

IV

The foregoing chapters highlight that forest-based industries should be set up in the tribal belt of India which would ultimately boost their economic condition. Some of such forest-based industries are: saw mills, charcoal processing, manufacture of plywood, pulp and paper industry, kendu leaf processing, cocoon or *kosa* processing centre, resin, gum making centre, *sabai* grass for thatching collecting centre, *phooljharu* making centre, honey packing, *kusum* seed, sal seed and *mahua* seed processing, preparation of *katha* or catechu, forest-based distilleries out of *mahua*, fruit processing centre (since mango, guava and custard apple are abundant in Bastar), rope preparing centre out of bark, tamarind collection and selling centre, mushroom and *chiraunji* processing centre, *sindoor* seed collection and processing centre, basketry manufacturing centre, wooden furniture manufacturing centre, and medicinal plant processing centre, etc. These are the core sector in forest economy by which forest-dwellers and tribal people are benefited. In this way, the fate of Indian rural economy along with the tribal economy will be elevated since the local ecosystem has contributed to welfare and living condition of rural people who have in many ways interlaced with forest. Therefore, forest-based tribal development and their participation in such programmes will lead to a unique pattern where the sustainable use of natural forest resources as well as the preservation-cum-conservation of ecosystem and biodiversity are also taken into consideration by the tribal people themselves, with the support of the government and the NGOs, for their survival.

Along with the mentioned developmental programme in the area of forest-based tribal habitation, the ecosystem or the immediate geographical environment may also be preserved in the following manner. In connection with plantation or social forestry in the forest area, the usable and edible fruit trees must be planted at the foot of hills for the use of forest-dwellers; such as, in case of Bastar area mango, guava, custard apple and cashewnut trees must be taken into consideration for plantation in the base of hills along with fuelwood. Above the foothills trees like *mahua, kusum, aonla, aden,* tamarind, jagdumar and some commercial trees must be planted and at the top of hills the commercial trees must be planted along with other trees whose roots can easily penetrate into the earth due to which they may easily stand erect on the ground even if they face any severe cyclonic storm. In this way, soil erosion will also be checked. This idea has been achieved after prolonged association with forest-dwelling tribes in various parts of our country and only in this manner the ecosystem can be properly balanced.

If we destroy the ecosystem, as well as biodiversities; we will destroy ourselves. All the flora and fauna of a geographical setting are important. Modern wars equipped with nuclear power technology not only destroy the life but also our natural ecosystem which ultimately in chain hampers our whole system. The natural environment and ecosystem will help us to develop our general health status and ability to cope up with various unknown diseases which are still found among various primitive tribes of our country; such as, Toto sores among Toto tribe of West Bengal, yaws among Abuj-Maria tribe of Bastar. More so, among Bastar tribes of Madhya Pradesh, there is dominance of sickle cell trait. The fatal disease yaws, is chiefly concentrated in Koraput district of Orissa, Bastar district of Madhya Pradesh and Khambam district of Andhra Pradesh among the tribal population. It is a kind of skin disease of syphilis type. The bacteria responsible for such a disease is *Tipanoma purtuni*; only one penicillin injection will cure it. Practically, in most of such cases the tribals are primarily dependent on herbs available in their niche. But due to thick forest in these areas the movement is restricted and in such forests the tribals like Abuj-Maria of Bastar live. In this regard, there is a proverb: "where road ends, this disease starts". Now one can easily understand about the rich natural resources and bio-diversities of our country in which Indian tribal people are closely interlaced in every sphere of their livelihood. Therefore, it is our duty not only to conserve the great cultural heritage of Indian tribes but also to conserve our rich biodiversities for our own sake.

Bibliography

Adhikari, A.K., 1984. *Society and World View of the Birhor,* Memoir No.60, Calcutta: Anthropological Survey of India.

Anderson, J.N., 1973. "Ecological Anthropology and Anthropological Ecology", in *Handbook of Social and Cultural Anthropology,* (ed.) J.J. Honnigman, Chicago: Rand McNally.

Banerjee, Biswanath, 1968. "The Habitat and Culture of Primitive Hill People of India", 21st International Geographical Congress, India.

Barth, F., 1956. "Ecologic Relationships of Ethnic Groups in Swat, North Pakistan", *American Anthropologist,* Vol.58, pp.1079-89.

Bates, M., 1953. "Human Ecology", in *Anthropology Today,* (ed.) A.L. Kroeber, Chicago: University of Chicago Press.

Bhowmick, P.K., 1989. *The Chenchus of the Forests and Plateaus: A Hunting-Gathering Tribe in Transition,* Calcutta: Institute of Social Research and Applied Anthropology.

Birdsell, J., 1953. "Some Environmental and Cultural Factors

Influencing the Structuring of Australian Aboriginal Populations", *American Naturalist,* Vol.87, pp.171-207.

Chandra, Ramesh, 1981. "Ecology and Religion of the Kinner", in *Nature-Man-Spirit Complex in Tribal India,* (ed.) R.S. Mann, New Delhi: Concept Publishing Co.

Conklin, H.C., 1954. "An Enthno-Ecological Approach to Shifting Agriculture", *New York Academy of Sciences, Transactions,* Vol.17, No.2, pp. 133-42.

Dasgupta, Samira, 1994. *Birjia: Society and Culture,* Calcutta: Firma KLM Pvt. Ltd.

Dasgupta, S.B., 1978. *Birjia: A Section of the Asurs of Chotanagpur,* Calcutta: K.P. Bagchi & Co.

Devarapalli, Jesurathnam, 1994. "Subsistence Systems and Limitations of Ethnoecology: A Case Study of Chenchus" in *Girijan Samskriti,* Vol.2, No.2.

Diener, P., 1974. "Ecology or Evolution? The Hutterite Case", *American Ethnologist,* Vol.61, pp.601-18.

Driver, W.H.P., 1889. "Notes on Some Kolarian Tribes", *Journal of Asiatic Society of Bengal,* Vol.LVII (I), pp.7-18.

Ellen, Roy, 1982. *Environment, Subsistence and System: The Ecology of Small Scale Social Formation,* Cambridge: Cambridge University Press.

Fernandes, Walter and Geeta Menon, 1987. *Tribal Women and Forest Economy: Deforestation, Exploitation and Status Change,* New Delhi: Indian Social Institute.

Frake, C.O., 1962. "Cultural Ecology and Ethnography", *American Anthropologist,* Vol.64

Forde, D., 1934. *Habitat, Economy and Society* (Reprinted 1979), London: Methuen & Co. Ltd.

Gazetteer of 1970 Bihar: *District Gazetteers : Ranchi,* India.

Geertz, C., 1963. *Agricultural Involution: The Process of Ecological Change in Indonesia*, Berkeley, University of California Press.

Gindi, Suresh Kumar, 1994. "Ethnomedicine Among the Yanadi: A Hunter-Gatherer Tribe in South India", *Girijan Samskriti*, Vol.2, No.2.

Grigson, Sir Wilfrid, 1991 (Reprinted). *The Maria Gonds of Bastar*, Delhi: Vanya Prakashan and Oxford University Press.

Guha, Uma, M.K.A. Siddiqui and P.R.G. Mathur, 1968. *The Didyai: A Forgotten Tribe of Orissa*, Memoir No.23, Calcutta: Anthropological Survey of India.

Hann, Rev. Ferd, 1900. "A Primer of the Asura Dukmar: A Dialect of Kolarian Languages", *Journal of Asiatic Society of Bengal*, Part I, p.149.

Hardesty, D.L., 1977. *Ecological Anthropology*, New York: John Wiley & Sons.

Harris, M., 1966. "The Cultural Ecology of India's Sacred Cattle", *Current Anthropology*, Vol.7, pp.51-61.

Haimendorf, C.V. Fürer, 1943. *The Chenchus: Jungle Folk of The Deccan*, London: Macmillan & Co Ltd.

Hajra, D., 1970. *The Dorla of Bastar*, Memoir No.17, Calcutta: Anthropological Survey of India.

Helm, J., 1962. "The Ecological Approach in Anthropology", *American Journal of Sociology*, Vol.67.

Jain, S.K., 1986. "Ethnobotany", *Interdisciplinary Science Reviews*, Vol.II, pp.285-92.

Jay, Edward J., 1968. *A Tribal Village of Middle India*, Memoir No.21, Calcutta: Anthropological Survey of India.

Knight, C.G., 1974. "Ethno-Science as a Research Paradigm", in *Language in Anthropology*, (ed.) W.C. McCormack and S.A. Wurm, Mouton: The Hague.

Kroeber, A.L., 1939. *Cultural and Natural Area of Native North America*, Berkeley: University of California Press.

—, 1969. "Relations of Environmental and Cultural Factors", in *Environment and Cultural Behaviour*, (ed.) A.P. Vayda, New York: The Natural History Press.

Leuva, K.K., 1963. *Asur: A Study of Primitive Iron Smelters*, New Delhi: Bharatiya Adim Jati Sevak Sangha.

Majumdar, D.N., 1961. "Foreword", in *The Sacred Complex of Hindu Gaya*, by L.P. Vidyarthi, New York: Asia Publishing House.

Milton, Kay (ed.), 1993. *Environmentalism : The View from Anthropology*, London: Routledge.

Nandan, A.P., 1993. *The Nicobarese of Great Nicobar*: An *Ethnography*, Delhi: Gyan Publishing House.

Negi, S.S., 1994. *India's Forest, Forestry and Wildlife*, New Delhi: Indus Publishing Company.

O'Malley, L.S.S., 1926. *Palamau District Gazetteer*, Patna.

Orlove, Benjamin S., 1980. "Ecological Anthropology", *Annual Review Anthropology*, 9: 234-73.

Prasad, Narmadeshwar, 1961. *Land and People of Tribal Bihar*, Ranchi: Bihar Tribal Research and Training Institute.

Rai, Suman, 1988. "Impact of Forest Policies on Forest Dwellers", *Social Welfare*, Vol.XXXV, No.8.

Rambo, A. Terry, 1983. "Conceptual Approaches to Human Ecology", *Research Report*, No.14, Honolulu Hawaii: East-West Environment and Policy Institute.

Ratzel, F., 1889. *Anthropogeographic*, Stuttagart: (Orig.1882) J.E. Engelhorn.

Rappaport, Roy A., 1963. "Aspects of Man's Influence on Island Ecosystem: Alteration and Control", in *Man's Place in the Island*

Ecosystem, (ed.) F.R. Fosberg, Honolulu: Bishop Museum Press, pp.155-74.

—1968. *Pigs for the Ancestors*, New Haven: Yale University Press.

—1969. "Ritual Regulation of Environmental Relations among a New Guinea People", in *Environment and Cultural Behaviour*, (ed.) A.P. Vayada, New York: The Natural History Press. Report of Scheduled Areas and Scheduled Tribes (Dhebar) Commission, Vol.I, 1960-61.

Risley, H.H., 1981 (Reprinted). *The Tribes and Castes of Bengal*, Calcutta: Firma Mukhopadhyay.

Roy, S.C., 1926. "Asur Ancient and Modern", *Journal of the Bihar and Orissa Research Society*, Vol.XII.

Roy Burman, B.K., 1968. "Forest and Tribals in India", in *Applied Anthropology*, (ed.) L.P. Vidyarthi, Allahabad: Kitab Mahal

Roy Chaudhuri, Bikash, 1980. *The Moon and Net: Study of Transient Community of Fisherman at Jambudwip*, Calcutta: Anthropological Survey of India (Memoir No.40).

Rajyalakshmi, P., 1991. *Tribal Food Habits*, New Delhi: Gian Publishing House.

Sahay, S. Vijoy, 1981. "The Nicobarese: A Study in Nature-Man-Spirit Complex", in *Nature-Man-Spirit-Complex in Tribal India*, (ed.) R.S. Mann., New Delhi: Concept Publishing Company.

Sahlins, Marshall, D., 1964. "Culture and Environment: The Study of Cultural Ecology", in *Horizons of Anthropology*, (ed.) Sol.Tax, London: Allen and Unwin Ltd.

Sahu, Nirmal Chandra, 1986. *Economics of Forest Resources*, Delhi: B.R. Publication Corpn.

Sandhwar, A.N., 1978. *The Korwa of Palamau: A Study of their Society and Economy*, Wien: Institute für Wolkerkunde der universitat.

Sarkar, Amitabha and Samira Dasgupta, 1993. "Study on Abuj Maria: A Primitive Tribe of Bastar", *Girijan Samskriti*, Vol.I, No.1.

—, 1993. *ToTo: Society and Change*, Calcutta: Firma KLM Pvt. Ltd.

—, 1995. "Ethnic Conflict: Unrest among Autochthons of Jharkhand", *Social Change*, Vol.25, No.4.

Sastry, V.N.V.K., 1995. "Empowering Forest Living Tribal Communities for Better Forest Management: Need and Opportunities", *Girijan Samskriti*, Vol.3, No.1.

Semple, E., 1911. *Influences of Geographic Environment*, New York: Henry Holt.

Singh, A.K., 1982. *Tribal Festivals of Bihar*, New Delhi: Concept Publishing House.

Singh, A.K. and M.K. Jabbi, 1995. *Tribals in India*, New Delhi: Har-Anand Publication.

Singh, G.S., 1997. "Socio-Cultural Evaluation of Sacred Groves for Biodiversity Conservation at Kullu District", *Man and Life*, Vol.23, Nos.3-4.

Singh, K.P., 1994. "Birhor: A Vanishing Tribe", in *Tribal Development Administration in India*, (ed.) Ashok Ranjan Basu, and Satish Nijhawan, Delhi: Mittal Publication.

Singh, K.S., 1994. *People of India*, Vol.III, *The Scheduled Tribe*, Delhi: Oxford University Press and Anthropological Survey of India.

—, 1996. *People of India, National Series, Vol.VII Identity Ecology, Social Organisation, Economy, Linkages and Development Process: A Quantitative Profile*, Delhi: Oxford University Press and Anthropological Survey of India.

Sinha, Rajiv K., 1991. "Ecosystem Preservation through Faith and Tradition in India", *Journal of Human Ecology*, Vol.2, No.1, pp.21-24.

—, 1995. "Contribution of Indian Tribals to Modern Civilization", in *Tribals in India*, (ed.) A.K. Singh and M.K. Jabbi, New Delhi: Har-Anand Publication.

Sinha, R.K., 1981. "A Note on the Nature-Man-Spirit Complex of a Tribe (Pando)", in *Nature-Man-Spirit Complex in Tribal India*, (ed.) R.S. Mann, New Delhi: Concept Publishing Co.

Smith, Robert Leo, 1972. *The Ecology of Man: An Ecosystem*, New York: Harper & Row.

Srivastava, A.R.N., 1990. "Rise of Ecological Studies in Cultural Anthropology", *Man in India*, Vol.70, No.3.

Steward, Julian H., 1955. *Theory of Cultural Change*, Urbana: University of Illinois Press.

—, 1968. "Cultural Ecology" in *International Encyclopaedia of Social Sciences*, Vol.14, pp.337-44.

—, 1968. "The Concept and Method of Cultural Ecology", in *Readings in Anthropology* Vol.II, (ed.) Fried H. Morton, New York: Thomas Y. Crowell Company.

Thamizoli, P., 1997. "The Sacred Grove of Kannimar the Irula Deity: An Insitu Conservation of Bio-diversity", *South Asian Anthropologist*, Vol.18, No.2.

Titiev, Mischa, 1955. *The Science of Man: An Introduction to Anthropology*, New York: Henry Holt and Co.

Toynbee, A.J., 1947. *A Study of History* (abridgement of Vol.I-VI), New York: Oxford University Press.

Vayda, A.P. and R.A. Rappaport, 1968. "Ecology: Culture and Non-Cultural", in *Introduction to Cultural Anthropology*, (ed.) J.A. Clifton, Boston: Houghton Mifflin Co.

Vayda, A.P., 1968. "Economic System in Ecological Perspective: The Case of the North West Coast", in *Readings in Anthropology*, Vol.II, (ed.) Fried. H. Morton, New York: Thomas Y. Crowell Company.

Vidyarthi, L.P., 1961. *Sacred Complex of Hindu Gaya*, New York: Asia Publishing House.

—, 1973-74. "Strategy for Tribal Development in India", *Adibasi*, Vol.15, pp.77-79.

Vidyarthi, L.P., 1981. "Foreword", to *The Profiles of the Marginal and Pre-Farming Tribes of Central-Eastern India*, (ed.) L.P. Vidyarthi, Calcutta: Bulletin of the Cultural Research Institute, Scheduled Castes and Tribes Welfare Department, Special Series No.26.

Wissler, Clark, 1926. *The Relation of Nature to Man in Aboriginal America*, New York: Oxford University Press.

White, Leslie, 1959. *The Evolution of Culture*, New York: McGraw-Hill.

Index